Growing up w
Autistic Brother

A Challenge and a Reward

Alexandra Amoroso

Growing up with an Autistic Brother

A Challenge and a Reward

Alexandra Amoroso

To my awesome, supportive, and loving parents Todd and Sheri Amoroso. Thank you for being so wonderful. You did and continue to do a wonderful job with Tony, taking great care of him.

In memory of our paternal grandmother Mary Amoroso Znosko who took care of Tony for my parents all of the time. He and I were the apple of her eye. She was a life saver for our parents.

"One person can make a difference and everyone should try."

John F. Kennedy

Introduction

Everyone is thankful for the siblings they have. Siblings can be annoying, frustrating, fun, and loving all at the same time. Unlike most children I grew up with a little brother who was diagnosed with autism. I learned a lot as a child, teen, and now adult of how hard life can get living with an autistic sibling but also, what a wonderful lesson it really taught me. As a child I was embarrassed of my brother, I was scared to have friends over, I was scared to go out in public and I was nervous when company came over. I didn't want anyone to not talk to me or think I'm different because of who my brother was. Later on I learned that my brother is the best thing that could have happened to me. He mainly taught me that every child in the world should be taught, that everyone is different each in their own way and that everyone should be accepted for the way they are. As I got older I knew there was only one thing that mattered to me and that was him. I had friends over, went out to family parties and other events. If no one could accept him for who he is they can walk out of my life. Truthfully, I am probably one of the luckiest people in the world. I am grateful every day for my friends and family who were always there to help my parents and me with my brother. This book is about none other than two children growing up together as siblings. However it was a bit different than any other ordinary family. I learned as many other children have learned what it is like to have an autistic sibling. I want to share with people all over the world what it was like growing up with a brother who was diagnosed with autism. It is something that is challenging and often times heartbreaking, but I wouldn't trade my life for anything in the world. My brother is everything to me and beyond that.

Chapters

Chapter 1

Big Sister

Who doesn't want to be a big brother or sister? Well I guess it is different for everyone. For me I didn't want a brother or a sister, I wanted to be an only child. I wasn't that excited when my brother was born like most children who were once an only child, but that soon changed for me. May 1, 2001 my mom went into labor early that morning. Later on while at my grandparent's house we got a call saying it was a boy. My brother was unnamed for a while. My parents had a hard time naming him. When we arrived at the hospital the badge on his crib read "Baby Amoroso". Later on my baby brother "Anthony Rosario Amoroso" was sitting in my lap. I remember looking down at him not as excited but happy to see that everyone else in the room was happy not only for my parents but for me as well. Three days later we took Anthony "Tony" as we called him home from the hospital. As a three year old I was never around a baby before and wasn't so sure what to expect. I got used to him very quick. I got used to his usual routine of napping, eating, and sleeping. I watched my mom and dad take care of him each day and also helped them in whatever way I could. As months passed my dad went back to work and my mom worked from home. One of my aunts and my dad's mom took me during the week to help my mom out while she was home with my brother. Tony was baptized in August of 2001. The whole family came to watch him be christened. For me, it was by far the most boring event I ever had to attend. I sat there impatient waiting for it to be over. After a while of sitting my dad held me next to my mom who was holding Tony so I could watch up close. I don't remember what we did afterwards, but I do know I couldn't wait to just get out of there. Tony got big month after month and became mobile very quick. He walked just before his first birthday and was interested in anything and everything like any other baby. His room was next to my room and across from my parents. It was red and yellow with a race car finish line pattern on the lower half of the walls. He had lots of pictures of Nascar especially Jimmy Johnson who was our papa's (mom's dad) favorite Nascar driver. Tony had a carpet on the floor in his room that looked like a city with roads and parking lots. Both of us had fun playing with his toy cars on the rug. Tony's first birthday party was big and was held inside because of rain the whole day. It was Elmo themed, he had Elmo table clothes, balloons, and more. When we sang happy birthday to him he sat in my grandma's arms (dad's mom) and wasn't so sure about everyone singing. Like any baby it was overwhelming. He had a big cake, it was chocolate with chocolate frosting. My mom cut a slice and gave it to Tony. The cake seem to hit every part of him except his mouth. Like any other birthday he enjoyed it. Tony and I never went to day care, we were lucky to have a mom who worked from home. On Tuesdays and Thursdays my dad's mom would take us when she got out of work at 2:00 pm. and kept us for the evening then my dad would pick us up after dinner or right after work. As a big sister I tried to help and guide Tony as a toddler. I remember helping him climb on the couch or onto the bed, and feeding him food, or help him get dressed. I had fun doing it and enjoyed his energy. We often both chased each other around the house which we thought was the best game ever until we got in trouble for making too much noise or breaking something which occasionally happened. In our living room we had a sectional couch which we were kind of rough on. When mom was at her desk and couldn't see us we would jump on the couch, run across it from one side to the other, and often go behind it where a tall lamp was to hide on each other. Again, it was all fun and games until we got caught. My brother and I knew what we were allowed to do and not do, and when we did something we knew we weren't allowed to do we paused in fear knowing mom was going to yell, or wait and tell dad when he got home from work. To be honest both scenarios scared us. A year passed and Tony turned two years old. I was young and didn't know and was unaware at the time but my parents noticed that Tony's behavior and actions were becoming rather strange. They noticed Tony became slow with a lot of things and couldn't keep up as much as I did at two. He also didn't really talk and hardly ever spoke in sentences. He was brought to be tested at the children's hospital where my parents were informed that Tony was diagnosed with autism. 1 in 88 children are diagnosed on the spectrum, making it hard for them to communicate and have social interaction. Tony started receiving services from Easter Seals Birth to 3 Program when he was two and did fairly well with it. He did different things every day and seemed to understand day after day how to do what. I was only five years old and didn't know what autism was and really didn't know Tony had it. I was confused at five and six years old as I watched my brother grow up and couldn't speak sentences like I did. I used to ask my parents each year if Tony would talk on his next birthday. I got used to Tony for who he was and went to a different school than him. He attended Hatton School in Southington because of their special education program and he did wonderful there. My parents knew he wouldn't be able to attend a public school like I did. Tony unlike most children was very hard to potty train. My parents tried each and every day and it took them forever. While at Hatton School his teacher and paras there kept Tony after school to help my mom potty train him. Tony soon got better at it during the day but at night was a different story. He would have accidents during the night giving my mom laundry to do almost every day. When he got older it never really changed. He would wet the bed at night even though we made him sleep in diapers and mom would keep a pad under the sheets so she didn't have to wash the mattress cover. His actions made it very difficult for my parents and mom and dad both realized that it was a little harder raising and teaching Tony things than it was when they had me. It wasn't Tony's fault at all. We like other families were about to learn the life of living with an autistic child. It is a big blessing and I cherish every minute I spend with Tony and every memory I have with him too. I thought being a big sister was both fun and challenging but when I got older and learned why Tony acted the way he did, it changed my childhood.

Chapter 2

The Obsessions

Every child has an obsession with a toy, a movie, a game, or a book. Tony had many different obsessions and they changed as years went on. My brother and I grew up watching Disney movies, Dream Works movies and Pixar. Most of the Disney movies came out when we were young and we watched every single one and we owned every DVD out there. My brother had some favorites, Disney movies it was: 101 Dalmatians, Beauty and the Beast, Snow White, Sleeping Beauty, Lion King, and more. Pixar was of course Toy Story and Toy Story 2, and his favorite movie from Dream Works was Shrek. Shrek was in the top five favorites, my parents and I can recite the entire movie without watching it. Tony watched it every single day. He also liked Shrek 2 but Shrek was his favorite. My brother not only had obsessions with these movies but with the characters and their actions in the movies. He loved the Disney princesses and I would often catch him in my room either wearing one of my skirts or dresses or taking my dolls off my shelves, my good dolls that I had for show and be playing with them. This annoyed me a lot. I would walk into my room and catch him there messing it up and making a mess in my closet and like any sister I yelled at him and made him get out. Tony and I never fought especially because he was non-verbal. However, when he made me mad that was it for me. As I kid I heard the same thing every single day from my parents. "He doesn't know any better". That frustrated me all the time, I thought as though well I know better, I know what I can play with and can't play with why doesn't Tony know? His obsession with Snow White was a little intense and at one point my parents didn't let him watch the movie. He would try and reenact the hunch man who was supposed to kill Snow White for the queen but didn't. Tony would sneak one of my mom's knives and reenact the scene with his stuffed animals. Luckily he didn't with one of us. My parents caught him one day and took the DVD away from him. His obsession with Shrek was quite funny. We watched Shrek about 50 times a day it felt like and Tony would find something in the house that looked like a bouquet of flowers and he would lay in his bed like Princess Fiona did while she waited for Shrek. When we were young our grandma Mary bought us a swing-set. It was perfect for my brother, he loved to swing and he would spend hours outside just swinging. It was easy for my mom too, her office was in the sun porch which had a view of the backyard so she was able to watch us play while she worked. I noticed when we were outside Tony would constantly play with a stick, he was obsessed with holding sticks. He wouldn't hit or hurt anyone or anything with the stick but he would walk around and carry it with him, sometimes swinging it or pretending it was a sword. His crazy obsession with sticks also led to his obsession with my mom's wooden spoons. Every night was the same, my mom or dad would start making dinner while Tony and I played in our rooms or watched television. Most nights however started like this... "Tony, where is my wooden spoon? Bring back here now!" One year for his birthday my mom bought him wooden spoons and wrote his name on them so her and my dad knew it was his. Our grandmother's oldest sister, our aunt Phil lived near us and often came over to see us. We always enjoyed her company and she was so wonderful with both Tony and I. Every time Aunt Phil would come by or my dad would go pick her up, she would walk in and put her cane by our back door. Well her cane wasn't there for very long, Tony would come out of his room to greet her and saw her cane in the corner it looked like a stick to him and he would walk around with it while he played. Of course Aunt Phil didn't mind at all. She enjoyed just watching Tony play. When I was little my favorite Disney movie was 101 Dalmatians, It was hard when I liked a movie that Tony didn't because he would be upset that we weren't watching the movie he liked. Taking turns wasn't one of his strengths as a kid, but he loved 101 Dalmatians also and he would sit with me in the living room and watch it. His obsession with this movie was collecting all our stuffed animals and tossing them to me on the couch like the Dalmatians did when they saved the puppies from Cruella De Vil. I enjoyed doing that with him, I found it fun to reenact saving all the puppies. His movie obsessions were just a start, from the time Tony was about 4 to 6 years old he was obsessed with wearing my mom's slippers and bathrobe. He would parade around the house in her bathrobe and slippers and he would do the same at grandma's house with her slippers and bathrobe as well. That obsession didn't last very long, I figured he was probably sick of wearing shoes that were ten times his shoe size. When it came time to eat dinner Tony was always very good about sitting down at the table, of course my parents trained him the same way they trained me and didn't baby him because of his autism. He was supposed to behave and be respectful just like me. Tony would sit down with us and behave, however he had a thing with certain foods. When he was young his meals consisted of meatballs, grilled cheese, pancakes, chocolate chip waffles, French fries, and chicken nuggets. He was a very picky eater, the only fruit he ever ate was an apple and he didn't like any vegetables until he got older. But even the food he did like had to be a certain way and if it wasn't he would know and not eat. My mom had to make his food a certain way for him, especially her meatballs. Tony didn't like the parsley in them, he would sit at the table or in his highchair and pull out every little piece of parsley he saw in the meatballs and then eat them. Sometimes it would take him hours just to pull all of it out. For snacks, his favorites were pretzels, goldfish, Granny Smith Apples, or chips. He once sat at the kitchen table and we were eating, dad asked Tony to try a peach and he refused. He kept saying no, dad said just one bite and you can have whatever you want. Well Tony took a bite and swallowed, I watched him closely and could see that he was going to puke. Dad grabbed him a bucket quick and he threw up the peach. That was the last time Tony had a peach. We were always happy when he did try something new. Tony always, from a little boy, loved sweets, his favorite cake or ice cream flavor however was chocolate. Mom one time bought an ice cream cake for someone's birthday, the next day mom cut Tony and I a piece of the cake. I ate the vanilla half of the piece and Tony ate the chocolate part of this then we switched plates. He gave me his vanilla and I gave him my chocolate. It was the little things that made us both happy. Food, toys, and clothes weren't even that bad for his obsessions. There was one obsession that drove me crazy. When we were kids I had a full size bed and Tony had a twin size bed, he ended up with a queen when he turned 9 years old but before then he thought big sister was going to share with him. Some nights I had no choice because I was sound asleep and didn't hear him sneak in. It started out of the blue, Tony figured out that my bed was bigger than his and he tried hard to take advantage of big sister's big bed. One night I was almost asleep when I heard my door open and heard no one talking so I looked and Tony was standing there waiting for me to invite him in. Well I sat up and said, "No

Tony go back to bed." He did go back if I was up to catch him. Some nights Tony found his way in my room and into my bed, then the next morning "surprise" there he was in my bed. I tried not to get mad but it highly annoyed me especially when I was already asleep and didn't know he got in my bed. His morning breakfast was either chocolate chip waffles or scrambled eggs. Every Tuesday and Thursday Grandma Mary would come and pick us up after work to take us back to her house. I would bring my homework and do it there. Sometimes she take us to Burger King and we were both excited. Especially Tony, he loved his French fries. Tony had his own routine even at grandma's house, he would walk inside grab a snack and went into the den to pick out what movie he wanted to watch. Grandma had all our toys and movies in her den, Tony would pick the movie and I would help him put it in. She had Elmo on DVD, Shrek 2, 101 Dalmatians, and others. I typically played with Tony or hung out downstairs with Poppy. Lots of times the night would go with Tony playing the same movie over and over, so I wouldn't bother him. I learned something and I learned it at a very young age, it was easier if Tony was still and quiet and if it kept him quiet I left him alone. I think the one thing that bothered me was that Tony had to do whatever I was doing, which wasn't really bad. I didn't mind, but when I played with my friends or with others sometimes he made it worse because he was different from me. He wouldn't play the game right or listen and I tried to include him like I was told and it was hard for me. There were times when I wanted him to let me be by myself. If I went outside to ride my bike he followed, if I went into the living room to play with my toys he followed, if I went downstairs to see poppy he followed. I didn't mind sometimes, but after a while it was very annoying. I felt sometimes I could never escape from him. A lot of my uncles and aunts took me out for the day or night so I had time to do things by myself, which was a treat for me. I wish Tony could have come with me and do things I did but he couldn't and it was tough for me. My brother was different from everyone else's siblings. He couldn't do the same things I did. It was challenging to keep track of him and every move he made. That was another reason it was easier to keep Tony at our house or grandma's because of his obsession with water. He loved to swim and grandma had a big pool at her house we would go in all the time. Tony was a great swimmer, that wasn't the problem, he swam great without a life jacket. The problem was keeping track of him to make sure he was 1) behaving in the pool and 2) that he didn't escape the yard; if he got bored in his own yard he would run off into the neighborhood. At grandma's it wasn't a big deal, her neighborhood was small and not busy. However, we live on a busy street and the one thing that everyone feared was Tony taking off into the street. He always played in the pool, our cousins came to our grandmother's house, friends and family and we had a blast in her pool; we thought her house was the best place in the world. No matter where we were or what time of the day it was Tony always asked to go swimming. He never left the hotel pools we went to, grandma's pool, or Uncle Paul's pool. He would constantly ask to go swimming no matter where he was or what time it was. In 2009 Poppy passed away that August. Grandma ended up selling her house the following year and moved in with us. Dad and mom extended our house and had an in-law apartment put in for grandma. When grandma moved in it was a big adjustment but Tony got used to it real quick. He loved every minute of every day that grandma was there. Although he didn't have a pool to go in... He had other ideas. Tony loved water, he was obsessed with swimming, in the ocean, a lake, or a pool. It didn't matter as long as he was swimming. A couple of our neighbors in back of us had swimming pools and once Tony didn't have a pool to swim in after grandma moved in, he quickly discovered all the neighborhood pools. We got a few phone calls from the cops about Tony going missing and after a while of trying to keep Tony in our yard, grandma finally convinced mom and dad to get a pool. We had a 24 foot wide round pool put in our yard. Mom and dad weren't really for it considering the house was still under construction from when grandma moved in in 2010. However, they had no choice grandma went out one day and came back telling them that people were coming over the next day to install a pool. Tony loved it and it did keep him in our yard, I had pool parties with my friends and cousins. It was a lot of fun. Dad and mom used it as well, even grandma did. Tony loved to go in the pool but he preferred to go in with another person. He didn't like to go by himself. That was a little hard for me, because I didn't always want to go in the pool. Even though my parents and I didn't like winter or the snow, it was one of the easiest seasons for us because Tony stayed in our house unless I helped him get in his snow suit and go outside sliding in the back yard. When Tony behaved he behaved, when he was bad, he was very bad. The one person who was able to handle and take care of Tony was Grandma Mary. Tony was good with her and he loved her, well... Why not? That was grandma, she gave us whatever we wanted and bought us whatever we wanted. Tony always sat with her and made sure she was somewhere in the house. He constantly went to her when he wanted something and he shared his bedroom with her while the house was under construction. In September of 2013 grandma died unexpectedly in our house while mom was getting ready for dinner. Grandma was rushed to the hospital where she was pronounced dead of a major heart attack. She never slept in her apartment, the day she died that morning we got her bed all ready for her and put the bed together. That night she would never sleep in it or see her apartment finished. The night she died people came in and out of our house mostly in shock. That night out of the blue I noticed Tony get his blanket, and stuffed animals and went into my grandmother's apartment. I followed him to see what he was doing, he got in grandma's bed and insisted he sleep there. I left the door open in case he decided to come back in his room but he didn't. He slept in her bed that night, and that was it. The next night he went back to his own bed. Tony may be autistic but there was no doubt in my mind at all he knew what happened that night. After grandma died I ended up stepping in and started getting Tony ready for school; mom and dad didn't ask me to do it I just did it on my own. He was my brother and I wanted to help out. Tony's breakfast obsession changed from eggs and waffles to a granola bar and a bowl of pretzels. When grandma moved in that's what he changed to because he knew she would give it to him, of course grandma would say, "it's pretzels, they're healthy" we couldn't break his obsession with that. Mom tried and made him eggs one morning and waffles but he wouldn't eat it. When Tony got older his obsession with watching television got worse and mom and dad ended up buying him a computer for his room where he would watch YouTube videos. The videos would make me crazy and it not only made me crazy but made Tony crazy too. He watch the movie or whatever and constantly rewind it over and over, he would never watch the full video and after a while he made himself crazy. We thought it would be good for him to have his own computer but, he became addicted and really never left his room after he got it. Shrek and Elmo were something we had to pull from Tony when he got older because for some reason watching it made him mad. We try not to let Tony watch them so much because we don't know how he will react to it. Tony's obsessions changed a lot from time to time, some days were harder than others but we took it as it went. His obsessions calmed down quite a bit since he has received a lot of help. As a little kid I couldn't understand why Tony was obsessed with a lot of different things. I only sat there as the big sister and watched him as he did what he did. As a teenager when I knew he had autism I really learned firsthand how it affected him. When I got older I did realize how easy it was to just let Tony watch what he wanted and play what he wanted to keep him quiet. Fighting with him was a complete waste of time. I couldn't really fight with him anyway because it was like arguing with a two year old. He didn't understand why I was mad or why I wanted to do it a different way. It was easier to let him get his way and other times it's a mistake. Sometimes his obsessions led to misbehavior, making it hard for us to redirect Tony.

Chapter 3

The Never Ending Tantrums

Nobody likes Mondays, room temperature coffee, being late, or forgetting your umbrella on a rainy day. Everyone has a bad day no matter what day it is or who it is, some days you're just in a mood all day long. It happens to all of us. Tony had his bad days almost every day, whether it was his clothes, his food, waking up, doing chores, not finding the right movie, or not wanting to do what he was told, it ruined his day. Tony threw tantrums as a child all the time, I did as well. However, I knew when to shut my mouth by a look mom gave me or when dad yelled. Tony wouldn't stop, it is understandable to me that Tony had tantrums a lot because he couldn't talk and couldn't express why he was upset. Every day it was something and it only got worse when he got older. Tony's tantrums didn't bother me when he was a toddler, it seemed normal to me. If he wasn't allowed to go swimming he would throw himself on the floor and throw a fit until somebody was able to redirect him to do something else. If he couldn't have a snack he wanted he would keep asking us until we couldn't take it anymore and yelled at him, then he would throw another tantrum until he gave up, which sometimes could be a long time. When we went on vacation one year to Old Forge, New York with our uncles and aunts and cousins on dad's side Tony behaved for one reason, because our hotel had an indoor pool. However, he wasn't such an Angel for very long. Our Uncle Frank was getting his boat ready for all of us to take a ride, our hotel was right on the lake where he parked his boat for us to take out. I was seven years old and Tony was four, dad helped us put our life jackets on and we got on the boat. Everyone was still getting ready and loading beach towels and coolers on the boat. Since we weren't moving yet Tony was getting anxious. He was tired of waiting and was trying to get off the boat, luckily he was a kid and dad grabbed him by his life jacket and held him in his lap until we were ready while Tony was kicking and screaming for the entire hotel and lake to hear. My aunt Evelyn and Aunt Lucille took some snacks out that they had packed and offered them to Tony, it distracted him until Uncle Frank got the boat going. Was I embarrassed? Not really, I was seven and to busy paying attention to my cousins who were with us. We were doing our own thing and fooling around until the boat was ready to go. Everyone in the family for the most part was amazing with Tony, he could cry, scream, and yell all he wanted and everyone understood, my dad's cousins and brothers were great with Tony. They would help my parents by taking Tony for a walk or getting him a toy and playing with him to distract him from his tantrums. Tony and I loved and adored Grandma Mary but, we also loved and always were excited to see our great- aunt Betty. She was our dad's aunt and Godmother. She was our paternal grandfather's sister. Our paternal grandfather "Nonno" died when dad was 12 years old, we never met him but both his sisters Aunt Betty and Aunt Faye were awesome ladies and they spoiled Tony and I worse than grandma did. Aunt Betty lived with dad's cousin, our Uncle Speedy as we call him and our Aunt Joyce. We went there a lot and they were great with Tony, he threw many tantrums there because he couldn't go in their pool, or didn't want what we were all having for dinner. They were great with him and their kids as well, if Tony was having a fit, someone would jump right in to give my parents a break and help them with Tony. One night we got invited to Uncle Speedy's house for dinner, I don't remember what exactly what was for dinner that particular night however, all I know was that Tony didn't want it. He yelled no multiple times, started to scream, and eventually threw himself on the floor because he wasn't eating. Aunt Betty came in from her room and asked why he was screaming; dad told Aunt Betty he'll be okay, and he just didn't like what was for dinner. Aunt Betty took Tony by his hand and took him to her apartment, dad and mom told her she didn't have to make him something but she did. She made him a grilled cheese and gave him pretzels. She was great with Tony and he loved her. She always had Hersey Kisses and other snacks on her kitchen table that Tony would take and she didn't care at all. It was wonderful how much the family loved Tony and cared about him, and treated him the same way they treated me. The tantrums only got more aggressive and louder as he got older though but they never bothered me really until I was in middle school. It annoyed me so much. I felt like I couldn't get away from it. I always looked forward to going out with friends and family without him so I could have a break and go have fun like any kid; not that I didn't want to have fun with Tony because I did and most times I did have fun doing things with him. We would play on the swing set, or our trampoline, we would play in the back of dad's truck, or ride our bikes around the driveway and deck. We would always have fun but when he had tantrums and would follow me everywhere it would start to annoy me. I didn't want to play with him all the time like any sibling. Tony did a lot of things to annoy me but his tantrums were enough for me. To be completely honest they made me nervous, and sometimes embarrassed and on top of it very furious. Every day my nerves were always on edge just because I never knew when he was going to have a tantrum. Every day we would sit in our rooms minding our own business, I would be on my computer and Tony would be on his and out of nowhere he would start yelling, screaming, banging his head and fists against the wall or even windows and it would just go right up my spine, my adrenalin would kick in and I would be so mad. I would run in screaming back at him which never made it better but it just set me off and I would yell. My parents told me all the time yelling makes it worse but there were many times when they yelled too, because he would just let out these blood curdling screams that could wake the dead. I would go back to my room and be mad. I would try to calm down even though he continued on with his screaming, it was just so unbearable for me. I hated every minute of it, it was the worst possible thing I had to listen to on a daily bases. When Tony was eight years old he was given a medication to help him sleep, although one of the side effects was eating, which made mom and dad end up getting a code lock for our pantry so Tony couldn't go in there any time he wanted. He also was put on clonidine to keep him calm. He also had Ativan that mom and dad gave him to calm him down when he would throw a fit. When grandma died I stepped in and helped my parents, most of the time my parents went out more than I did. I felt as though they were the parents and have to deal with Tony the most so I always offered to stay home with him while they went out to eat, or to a party, or out with friends. Just because my parents were out having a good time didn't mean they weren't worried about me being home with Tony by myself. My dad has even told people how nervous he would be, and he really was too. He would call constantly to see if I was okay and if Tony was behaving. Most times I watched Tony he really wasn't bad. When it got late he knew I meant business and I would give him his medication, have him put his pajamas on and I would tell him to shut his computer off it's time for bed. He usually listened and was on a good schedule. I learned something about Tony as I watched him throw certain tantrums over different things. I found that if we caught him early enough before he went into a full blown fit then he seemed a little easier to redirect quickly, but if he started and he was really having one, there was no stopping him. He would just continue either until he would decide to stop which sometimes lasted over a half an hour or 45 minutes, unless we gave him something to calm him down quicker. Mom and dad went out to one of their friend's house one Friday night and I stayed home with Tony. It was going fine for a while he was in his room and I was in the living room watching television. An hour goes by and it starts... I heard Tony hit something in his room, as I sat there rolling my eyes I got up and went into his room to see what the problem was. Tony was watching one of his normal movies, I turned it off and told him to take a break; he yelled no and still continued to scream. I could feel my blood pressure rising, I calmly said again to him, "Tony take a break for a while." When he screamed again I lost it, I slapped him across the face and yelled back at him. "Just shut up and walk away if it is bothering you!" "You are the worst brother ever, why did I get stuck with you!" "You do nothing to make my life easy!" I walked out slamming his door in anger, he continued to cry and he cried for a while I opened the back door and went outside on the deck and sat down. I wasn't going back inside until he was absolutely quiet, the screaming was just unbearable it went up my spine and was just something that can make you really, really mad. I didn't even go in to give him medication, because I didn't want to listen to him scream for one more second. After about 15 minutes I went back inside and walked down the hall to Tony's room, he was laying on his bed and he looked at me. I said, "Are you done?" He replied, done. I said, "Okay come get some water and relax for a while and then find something different to watch." After I got him water and put on a different movie for him, he calmed down. Around 7:00 or 7:30 I would normally give Tony his medication so it would start to kick in and around 9:00 or a little after. I would ask him to shut off the computer and go to bed. He usually always listened to me when it was time for bed, he knew when it was time. Every once in a while we could get through a day without Tony having a tantrum; this typically occurred when Tony would be doing other things instead of sitting at his computer all day. If he was able to either go swimming, jumping on the trampoline, or swinging on the swings he would blow off a lot of energy and wouldn't be as high strung. When I became a teenager and understood more about Tony's autism, a lot of times at night I would go to bed and lay there for a while staring at the ceiling and just thinking why he has tantrums? What sets him off? Is he mad at someone at school or home? I constantly questioned it and always wondered why it would happen. I do really believe a part of it is that Tony couldn't talk so when he is mad he has no other way to express his feelings other than scream like he does. I also wondered if his screaming was triggered sometimes by a bad dream; not all the time but once in a while Tony would wake up in the middle of the night crying and screaming at like two or three o'clock in the morning, waking the whole house up of course. Mom would get up and give him one of his Ativan with water and sit with him for a few until he calmed back down. As a child he never screamed in the middle of the night, it started when he got older once in a while. I used to stop and think I wonder if he had a bad dream and it scared him that bad. Tony used to get home from school about a half hour or so after me and believe me I enjoyed every second of quiet during that half hour. If mom and dad were both working I would normally wait for Tony to get off the bus. This one particular day in the spring of 2014 I had another thing coming for me when Tony got off the bus. I was waiting for Tony on the front porch, when his bus pulled up and I heard him screaming from inside his bus. My heart sank and I was scared of what would happen because he had to get off the bus and get in the house. I was scared he would run in the road or not come up the drive way and I was home all by myself. His bus driver and aids were the nicest people and were so understanding and patient with Tony. I wasn't embarrassed because they were so nice, however I was scared of what Tony's actions would be when he got off the bus. I sat on the porch wondering what to do. Tony got off the bus and threw his back pack on the drive way. He then threw himself on the driveway while he screamed and cried. Now there was no way 103 pound me was going to get my 250 pound and six foot brother in the house. I called mom crying and told her what happened. Mom said she was about 40 minutes away from home and wouldn't be able to get there any time soon. Mom told me if he continues to call 911 and have them take him. I hung up with her and sat on the porch sobbing knowing whether I go down there and yell at him or scream back it won't make the situation any better. I sat on the porch and opened my phone... I began to dial 9-1-1. I watched as he was still lying on the driveway kicking and screaming and I put my phone down. I just didn't have the heart to call and have Tony taken away, I couldn't do it, and I didn't want to do it. What if Tony knew I did that to him and he knew it was me? What if they couldn't get him in the ambulance and had to call for more help? I just didn't want to see any of that. I sat and waited I didn't move at all. After about 10 minutes he got up grabbed his back pack and walked up to me. I looked at him and told him I was upset with him then told him to get into the house and go to his room. He did his usual thing after school, where he put his back pack away and his lunch box, grabbed a snack, and then went to his room. I sat down on the couch wondering again, why? Why did it happen? Did someone in school make him mad? Did something happen on the bus? What caused him to come home like that? I was mad deep down and kind of embarrassed as cars drove by and saw him lying there screaming, but I also felt bad for my brother because that is all he knows. Of course mom and dad felt bad for both of us and tried to rush home to help me, but were proud of the way I handled Tony and to be honest I am just thankful that I know how he is and I could handle him. The one reason I watched Tony most of the time was, we couldn't just get any babysitter off the street to watch him, and it was a full time job and a hard one too. His obsessions weren't the problem at all, trying to calm him down and keep him calm was not just a challenge for me but also my parents. There were a lot of times where mom and dad lost their patience with Tony and have yelled and screamed back, and there were also times where he would make my parents nervous as well. In April of 2014 mom fell and broke her ankle in two different places, she had to stay off her foot for three months. She used a wheelchair to get around the house and crutches as well. Dad and I were on top of things as much as possible and my mom's parents would come over to help with cleaning and laundry that had to get done. One day while dad was at work, packing up and getting ready to come home, I was home with mom and Tony. Mom was in the recliner on her laptop doing work and Tony was in his room; out of nowhere Tony starts one of his tantrums and this tantrum wasn't like any tantrum he had. He was mad beyond mad and again we didn't know why. I ran down to his room because mom couldn't get up and I quickly turned off his computer which didn't help at all. I tried to redirect him and calm him down, but nothing was working. At the time, because grandma died, mom was receiving visits from Wheeler Clinic and DCF to talk about getting services for Tony and possibly finding a group home for him down the road. Mom and dad were told about this number to call instead of 911; the number was 211 and they are supposed to come out like 911 does and help you with your special needs child. I was crying because he was making me nervous and dad was on his way home so he wasn't there to help me or mom. Mom got on the phone and decided to try calling 211. She explained the situation and held the phone out so they can hear Tony screaming. They said someone would be out to the house soon. Meanwhile dad comes home and he can't calm Tony down either. He just screamed and screamed while destroying everything he owned in his bedroom. He banged on the walls, was throwing books, toys and hitting himself. He just wouldn't stop. Dad caved and gave him an Ativan to calm him, but this time it took a while to kick in. Well 45 minutes go by and nobody showed up at the house.

Finally, when the lady did show up, she sat at the kitchen table with my parents asking them questions while Tony was still screaming even with his medication in him. Dad had enough and asked the lady to go down the hall and do something with Tony, we called them to help us with him not to sit and talk about his life. By the time the lady was done talking to us, she went down to see Tony but he had already calmed down. Dad and I were furious but we couldn't leave because mom couldn't get up and move. The women left and we never ended up calling 211 again. Mom sat with me and said if you really need help with your brother and dad and I aren't here, then just call 911. It was just a complete joke. My whole life I went through my days wondering how and why Tony did what he did. What triggered it? Why was my brother autistic? Why do I have to go through these toddler tantrums every day of my life? I was scared in elementary school to have friends over. I begged mom and dad to bring Tony to Grandma Mary's and they did. I was young at the time and they did it for me so I can have friends over once in a while. Grandma always took him and she understood as well. I just didn't want to have to explain to my friends why he did what he did and in elementary school I shouldn't have to; I was little and just wanted to have playdates with my friends by myself. When I went into middle school and high school I not only had a brother with special needs but I attended a school with kids that are special needs and of course I don't care who it is everyone should be treated the same way. It was then I realized that I should have friends over with Tony home because I finally said to myself, if my friends or anyone who comes into my home can't respect my brother for who he is then they can walk out my door and never come back. My brother deserves the same treatment and respect that I get. All my friends knew Tony was autistic and I did explain to them that he can be loud and may scream or have a meltdown. My friends have got to be by far the best people I have ever met in my life. My friends are always so kind to my brother and words cannot express how much I appreciate that. Of course Tony is very kind too, he always says hello to them when they come to my house. I am very blessed with the friends I have, they are very nice to my brother and if he is having a moment they try and cheer me up because they see that it bothers me, but they have never judged me or my brother and I that is just what true friendship is. Despite the fact that Tony's tantrums were hard to deal with and annoying when he had one almost every day, when relatives or friends offered to take me out or my grandparents, I took full advantage, not because I didn't want to be with my brother, but because it gave me a break. I felt bad when he would have big tantrums because I would yell at him and tell him I hate him and that he was the worst thing that ever happened to me. In those moments I was beyond upset and annoyed by his random outbursts that I just don't know why he does that. Each time I would say it, but in the end I would go in when he calmed down and say I'm sorry but also let him know how mad I was, because Tony isn't dumb and we both know that, he just can't verbalize his feelings. He knows when I am mad and why I am mad and I always let him know why I am mad at him. Just because he annoyed his big sister didn't mean that everyone else in the world could judge him or feel annoyed, I will hurt anyone who makes fun of my brother or tries to judge him. No one knows and I mean NO ONE knows what it is like to live with an autistic child until you have lived with one. Despite Tony's random tantrums that can wake the dead and get on every single nerve in your body, I didn't and still don't let that ruin my relationship with my brother. I will always be there for him whenever he needs me despite the never ending tantrums.

Chapter 4

Attempting to Travel

There is nothing more fun for any kid or adult than traveling, whether it is a day trip, a weekend getaway, or a couple of weeks away. It is something everyone looks forward to. For me, I traveled but not as much as most kids because mom and dad's nerves would be on edge, not knowing how Tony would behave or react to different situations. We always have described Tony's tantrums as being a time bomb, no one ever knew when he would have a tantrum or not. When we took a day trip to our grandparent's house or aunt and uncle's house or a cousin's house it was easy. Everyone knew how Tony was and didn't have a problem with him at all, but as I have said many times, sometimes it was just easier to leave him with a sitter, not because we didn't want Tony to come with us but because we had to watch every move he made, making it hard to relax when we were out whether we were with family or not. Our whole family is great with Tony but even they do not know what it is like to live with him 24/7. The one good thing is Tony was and still is very good in the car. He loves car rides whether they are long or short. However, lots of times where ever we went it was usually a last minute decision especially if it was out in public. This one day when we were kids my mom and our great-grandma Louise wanted to take Tony and me out to lunch at Friendly's. I was seven years old and Tony was four. At first it went very well. After a while Tony started to get very antsy, he began to have a tantrum and not listen to mom, I could tell mom was a little embarrassed. She quickly got him up and took him to the car, Nana and I looked at the menu then Nana told me to go ask mom if she wants her to order the food to go. Mom was fine with that, so we waited for the food and went back to our house to have lunch. Mom felt bad for both Nana and me but Nana understood and didn't mind at all, she was very good with Tony and often helped my mother babysit us together with no problem; now that I look back at that I realize how amazing my mom's grandmother was. When we took Tony out and he was good, we felt good and had more courage to try and take him out more, but not every time we all went out was the greatest. It all depended on his mood that particular day. We even attempted family vacations a few times and each time wasn't that bad at all, like I said, Tony loves being in the car and if there were activities like the beach and a pool or a park he had fun with all of us and it made him tired by the end of the day which was great because he went right to bed. In the summer of 2005 we all took a family vacation to Old Forge, New York where my dad's brothers had a boat on the lake up there. We stayed five nights and six days, it was a lot of fun. Our hotel was right on the water where they had the boat parked, the hotel had a pool, and there was a water park across the street from the hotel. The ride up was about five hours or so and Tony of course was always good in the car and we did stop along the way in between. A couple of our cousins were there and we had the best time, it was fun for all of us kids. The first day we were there, we were going for a ride on the boat. At the time I was seven and Tony was four, my mom gave me my life jacket and helped Tony get his on. Tony was getting antsy because we were waiting for the adults to get everything they needed to bring on the boat. He wanted to get off because we weren't going anywhere just yet, dad grabbed him by his life jacket and made him sit next to him until we were ready to go. Tony didn't like it and did throw a small tantrum because he wasn't getting his way. After a few minutes everyone was ready and my uncle started the boat and we left the dock by the hotel, once we were moving Tony was at ease because we weren't just sitting there. Tony was great on our boat ride, he actually fell asleep and slept a while on the boat. Mom and dad were very happy and seven year old I just enjoyed being there with my cousins and uncles and aunts. It was great and I think everyone was happy that Tony was enjoying it too. He loved the hotel pool, it was an indoor pool and there was a deck outside so the adults were able to sit and watch him from the deck. The second day there we all decided to go try the water park across the street, mom and dad brought a stroller for Tony. There was a park and a water park, they had a princess that told stories, kind of like an enchantment kind of thing. The water park didn't really go as we expected. We got to the water park and we all stayed together, it was very busy there. Near the front of the park there was a pirates cave that had pirates in it and it told a story when you went inside. We had a lot of fun, mom and dad let Tony out of his stroller and we ran back and forth out of the cave, dad was on one end scaring us as we came out. Each time we came out it was me, my cousin Riely, and Tony. Dad kept on watching as the three of us ran in and out. Well, after a while of doing that dad saw only two kids come out, Riely and me. Dad then stopped looked at mom and my Uncle Joe and said, where is Tony? Mom and my Aunt Lucille went back in the pirate cave and there was no Tony. We lost him; autistic or not that is every parent's worse nightmare when they have lost their child in a busy place. My mom and Uncle Joe went one way, my dad went another way, and my Aunt Lucille stayed with Riely and I so they didn't lose us next. I was young and only knew that Tony was missing. Now, when I look back, I can't imagine the panic and pain my parents were feeling that day. At the time Tony went through a faze where he would like to take off his shoes and he took them off no matter where he was. He enjoyed going barefoot more than anything, which he did a lot. At one of the princess's castles in the park mom found Tony's shoes on the ground in the castle; she called down to dad saying she had his shoes. Dad's initial reaction was that someone could have kidnapped him which made him even more nervous than he already was. Dad ran towards the exit to try to talk to one of the security guards there to get help. As dad got to the exit of the park, he heard a bunch of commotion behind him; when he turned and looked he saw Tony walking across the train tracks they had for the train rides barefoot. Dad immediately ran towards him and grabbed him. It was sad to see the people there waiting for the train just staring at Tony and not trying to help him or to look for his parents. Dad ran to find mom, Uncle Joe, Aunt Lu, and us. At this point mom and dad had enough and thought it was best to take Tony back to the hotel to just swim in the pool where they can relax and keep a close eye on him. Dad and my Uncle Frank and Aunt Evelyn took Tony back to the hotel and mom, Aunt Lu, and Uncle Joe stayed with Riely and I for a little while longer at the water park. It was a big experience for not only Tony but for my parents and I as well and after that we took a lot of precaution when bringing Tony to public places. The rest of that vacation was fine as we just kept him by the pool and the lake where it was easier for us to watch him with less people around. Traveling was a big toss up, it was either really easy to do with Tony, really hard, or in the middle. For most parties and family events my parents always hosted them and had them at our house which made it easier for Tony to be in his own home and it was easier for mom and dad, not having to worry about his behavior at someone else's house. As a child I was fortunate to take the vacations and other trips I did take. However, I didn't get to go to a lot of faraway places which I used to be upset about as a child but now when I look back I do realize why we didn't; because mom and dad were scared to take Tony on a plane. He could have a tantrum on the plane or get antsy and try to walk around and there would be nothing mom and dad could do because we would be inside a plane thousands of feet in the air. It just made them nervous, every thought about it, and vacation isn't supposed to be about being nervous, it's about having a good and relaxing time. In July of 2006 my parents, my dad's cousins, my cousins, and Tony went on a vacation for eight days to the Outer Banks, North Carolina. It was probably one of the best vacations we ever took and Tony was very good on this vacation. Grandma Mary and Auntie Betty also came along with us, two of Tony's favorite people. It was about a 10 hour drive. Tony was great in the car. We had a portable DVD player for Tony and I to watch movies while we were in the car. There were 12 of us on vacation, making it easy to keep Tony busy throughout the vacation. This vacation was one of Tony's best traveling experiences. Our bedroom had two bunk beds, I slept in one above Auntie Betty and Tony slept in the other one above grandma. Tony was always good for grandma and Auntie Betty because they gave him whatever he wanted and did whatever he wanted. Tony loved every minute of the whole vacation. Our house was about a two minute walk to the beach and there was a wagon in our garage. Dad put Tony and me in the wagon and we would go to the beach. Tony loved the water and there were enough people to watch him in the water. For mom and dad it was a relaxing vacation with the help they had from everyone and the fact that Tony napped some days after playing in the pool or ocean all day. The ride home was rough for dad, Tony at one point was getting antsy and wouldn't listen to mom so he kept kicking dad's seat while he was driving. Dad was really mad and probably wanted to strangle him. Thank God we had that portable DVD player and once we put Tony's favorite show on he calmed down, even if we had to watch it over and over until we got home, it kept him quiet. As Tony got older it was getting harder to take him out because he was getting bigger and at some point dad couldn't pick Tony up off the ground while he was having a tantrum. We never went out for that reason, it scared us to even try and attempt to bring him out in public. My parents would just be paranoid the whole time not knowing if Tony would behave or not. However, taking Tony to the store got a little easier especially when mom had to buy his snacks. Tony did and still will do anything for pretzels or Smart Food popcorn. Mom would put them in the cart and would tell him to be good or he wasn't getting his snacks. He did well holding on to the shopping cart and staying by moms side for those snacks he really wanted. Mom and dad enjoyed having the family over because at one time when we were kids everyone was close. Mom and Dad would have everyone over making it easier because they knew Tony was safe and behaving; it was good because Tony was at home where his room, toys, and movies were so he was calm. He loved seeing the family all the time, everyone had fun with him and always played with him and included him in everything. After receiving some help and services for Tony, it was easier to take him out. He became calmer and wanted to go out to get out of the house like any other teenager. I got my license when I was 17 years old and the rule was I couldn't drive with Tony for six months, which was kind of a downer because I thought it would great if I took him out of the house for a while so mom and dad could relax. When I was able to take Tony out on my own it was nice, the only problem was it was hard for me to find a new place to take him each time. I only took him to the park for him to blow off steam and I would take him to Burger King or McDonald's because it was easier for me to go through a drive thru, not knowing how Tony would act if I actually took him into a restaurant by myself. I was too scared to do that. It helped to take him out but was also hard trying to find a place where I knew he would be okay and I wouldn't have to fight him to get back into the car. It was always nice when we could take a family trip or a ride somewhere when Tony behaved. We weren't always that lucky though.

Chapter 5

Handling and Understanding my Autistic Brother

My childhood wasn't like any ordinary childhood, it was different, very different. I often wondered why it was the way it was for me but none of the other kids I went to school with. When I got older and Tony got older, handling him was difficult for me, he always made me nervous. I never knew when he would have a fit and when he would get frustrated with something. I knew a tantrum was coming on and I honestly never knew how to react. Sometimes, I would yell because I usually lost my patience with him. Other times I would leave the house and go outside until he was done screaming whether it was in the middle of winter or on a hot summer day. I tried to put my headphones on but his screaming was so loud it would go right through my music. I will admit, I was never any good at handling Tony when he got crazy because I could have slapped him right across the face and yelled "what the hell is wrong with you?" It wasn't easy for me at all and it still isn't, once he gets something in his head that he wants he will ask over and over for it until someone gives it to him and it is by far the most annoying thing. I used to never understand why he would just be quiet after we said no the first time. For me since I was young if mom and dad said no, it meant no and I wouldn't keep asking. Of course Tony didn't understand that, he always had a one track mind, he wanted what he wanted when he wanted it. Some people never understood how hard it was not just for the parents but for me. When you are sitting calmly at your desk, on the couch, in the kitchen, or on your bed relaxing and doing your own thing and all of a sudden you hear banging and screaming coming from your brother's bedroom. It's not easy to constantly live with, the damage he caused breaking glass, his bedroom windows, taking his door off the hinges, and just banging his fists or his head against something was scary to not only hear but to witness. Out of everyone in the house mom could handle Tony the best when these outbursts happened and when mom lost her patience Tony knew he crossed the line with her. Mom has yelled and lectured Tony many times from his childhood to his teenage years. Honestly my parents, Tony's teachers and helpers, and I believe his tantrums only got worse as he grew up because for one he was going through puberty, two when something goes wrong or if he is upset and sick he can't tell any of us what is wrong with him and three every teenager enjoys being with friends and taking trips out because they are of age to do things by themselves and Tony was always trapped in his room just watching movies on his computer. Now when I look at that and think, I would probably go crazy myself if I couldn't do anything. If I was able to redirect my brother, to change the movie he was watching or to focus on something else, I was having a great day because he actually listened to me and made the decision to take a break rather than have a meltdown. However, I was never always this lucky. Some days all I would do is redirect Tony over and over again. For some reason when he got older his a couple of his favorite movies like Toy Story, Shrek, and Elmo made him anxious and he would get stimulated by it. When I would start to hear him getting aggravated, I would go to the computer and change it which was a challenge. He would scream "No, no, no!" which made me even more mad because he is obviously not enjoying the movie so why watch it? "No Tony pick something else to watch." I said to him firmly. When he said no again I gave him some choices. "Lion King, Monsters INC, or 101

Dalmatians?" When he chose one and was redirected, he calmed down. Tony knows how to work the computer and tablet, he just doesn't know how to spell so he can't type anything in to watch something. Mom finally blocked a couple of things on YouTube that made him crazy like Elmo and Shrek. Little did we know Tony was smarter than we were; somehow he managed to find Elmo or Shrek. My brother may be autistic but he is very smart. For me as a teen, a lot of times I felt trapped in my own home. I felt as though I should help out with Tony and also take some responsibility to give my parents a break. I really never invited friends over because Tony's random outbursts scared me and I didn't go out as much either because in grade school and middle school I was afraid people would say something to me about Tony or make fun of me for having an autistic brother. I got bullied myself in school for being blind in one eye. Some kids on the bus would make fun of me for it and cover one eye to look at me. It worried me what they would possibly say or do to my brother. I always remember just being nervous, I was never nervous in school because I knew Tony was well taken care of at his school, but I felt very nervous all the time. What if he has a fit while mom and dad aren't home? What if he gets out of the house and I can't find him or get him back home? I didn't have a constant eye on Tony but I would check on him frequently to make sure he was okay and calm. Usually when I was home alone with Tony I would always check to make sure he was watching something that he actually enjoyed, something that didn't make him over stimulated. If Tony was having a good day, I was having a good day. While Tony sat in his room on his computer watching his movies and shows I would sit in my room with my door open so I could hear him or I would sit and watch television in the living room. Tony would make his way out of his room once in a while to ask me for a snack. He wasn't able to have many snacks because the medication he took would make him hungry and he would just eat and eat. He typically ate pretzels or a granola bar for a snack. If we felt as though he had enough we would say, "Have an apple Tony." Apples were the only fruit he ate, even if he had 5 or 6 a day we let him because it was healthy. Sometimes Tony would come out and sit next to me on the couch to watch something. It was hard to find something we both liked because as I got older I was into history and documentaries and Tony still watched Disney movies or Sesame Street. Most people probably think that is crazy or weird but it was all because of his autism. He was just used to his regular movies and shows he watched as a child. At night Tony wasn't that hard to deal with, he would get into his pajamas and take his medications. He had some time to watch what he wanted to before bed. When we came in to tell him to shut his computer off he usually always listened. By this time his meds had kicked in a little bit and he was feeling tired anyway. Every parent and sibling knows and remembers waking up every hour of the night with an infant. Tony didn't do this all the time, but when he got older there would be some nights every once in a while where he would wake up screaming at 2 a.m. or 3 a.m. We don't know if he had a bad dream or he was hot because he couldn't tell us, but occasionally this would happen. Mom would get up and go try to calm him down. If he didn't calm down she give him one of his Ativan and he would go back to bed. Even in the middle of the night we still do not know what Tony's reason was for these tantrums. It was just as frustrating for us as it was for him because we didn't know what was bothering him and he couldn't tell us. Was I an expert at handling my brother every time I had to? Absolutely not, I was never a "know it all" with Tony or tried to tell people how to handle children with autism, I wasn't a professional at it at all. I still can't always handle him in his worst moments. Sometimes he would work with me, calm down, and focus. Other times, I would have to walk away because if he wouldn't listen I just wanted to slap some sense into him until he stopped and focused. It is the hardest thing ever, harder than school, harder than work, harder than anything. It was the most difficult thing to sit there with my brother who is crying and I am useless. I have no way to help him because he can't tell me why he is upset and deep down inside each tantrum he had, it broke my heart. I am no professional at all, but I was always there for him because that was all I could do for him.

Chapter 6

The Life of the Sibling

Every parent of an autistic child plays a big and important role in their life. Their job is harder than anything. I know because I watched my parents do that job. The sibling of an autistic brother plays a few roles. The helper, the guider, and the learner. There are many times where you have no choice but to step in and help out. For me, I helped out with a lot. Chores had to be done and I had to do most of them. Tony would put his clothes away and empty the dishwasher if you asked him. Most of the chores were for me because Tony couldn't do them. If Mom and Dad were out for the night, or if I was the first one up in the morning with Tony, I had to know how to give him his meds. I had to know which ones were for morning and which ones were for night, and when to give them to him. He was never allowed to get them himself, and we never showed him how, only for safety reasons. If Mom and Dad were both at work, and no one was home to get him off the bus, I was there. I had no choice. I couldn't go out until they got home because he couldn't get in the house himself or be by himself. Tony was always a picky eater. His meals after school consisted of grilled cheese or meatballs. Mom always made meatballs in advance and kept them in the freezer to throw in the microwave for him. I would always make sure he had dinner at a reasonable hour if he was home with me. He would get the meatballs for me and put them in a bowl. Then I would do the rest. Even though I had no choice but to help out a little more than my share with him, I did it. I didn't mind getting him his snack or helping him out with the things he needed. My parents did all of that for him when he was younger. I at least did it for them so they can have a break. Mom has said to a lot of people that Tony always listened to me more than them. At a certain point in my childhood, I realized I was also a guide to my brother to show him how to do certain things and to tell him right from wrong. Tony understood some of it and knew what was dangerous. He knew what was okay to do and what wasn't, but like any kid, he tested my parents. If Mom and Dad weren't in the room, and he was doing something I knew wasn't good, I didn't sit there and watch. I told him "no..." many times in my life. I would say, "No Tony that is Mom's" or "Tony that isn't yours, don't touch." A lot of my guidance was for his own safety. As a kid, I fell off of my bike many times, tripped on the driveway while running, got stitches in my foot from dropping a glass bowl on them, and much more. After getting hurt so many times, the phrase "safety first" sticks in your head before you do something. There were many times I caught Tony climbing on top of his tall dresser, standing on top of the couch or chair, and running with a glass in his hand. If I saw it, I would tell him, "No, you're going to get hurt." Even though Tony was autistic, he and I did get into some trouble together, and we both knew it too. In my bedroom, I had a full size bed with a canopy on it. It had three bars going across to hold it up and Tony and I would climb onto my foot board and swing from one bar to the other and land flat on the bed. We did it all of the time while Dad was cooking in the kitchen or Mom was at her desk and when someone came down the hall, we stopped and acted like we were just playing with our toys. Eventually, we both got caught when the bars on my bed were bent from us swinging. Dad and Mom weren't happy, but they got over it. Dad ended up taking my canopy down and I moved on to a regular headboard and footboard. Did I regret doing it? No, it was a lot of fun. My brother couldn't talk, but I knew he didn't regret it either. We had a blast while it lasted. It gave us a fun thing to do together when we were stuck in the house. Tony didn't cooperate and listen all of the time, that's for sure. I learned a lot from having this experience with a sibling with special needs. Tony and I were both very different in many ways and in everyone else's eyes. I think it was hard for me to understand that Tony couldn't do everything I did or understand the things I now understand. Every time I got frustrated with Tony, I always got the same response, especially coming from my grandparents which was, "he doesn't know any better" or "he doesn't understand that." It was always Tony's words over mine because for one, he didn't talk and two, everyone always assumed it was me annoying him. I also learned something very quickly at a young age. I learned that parents don't care at all about justice. All they want is quiet. I never took Tony's toys because I had my own and we were both into different toys as kids. When he came into my room to take mine, I used to get mad. Even when I wasn't home, I knew when he took one of my toys. If I went into Tony's room to get what was mine and he had it, World War Three was about to begin. Tony would yell, "No, mine!" I would fight back yelling it was mine. Once I took it, I left him in his room screaming and crying. When I would go into my room and close my door, a few seconds later, I would usually hear someone coming down the hall. Mom would open my bedroom door and ask why she heard Tony and me yelling. When I explained the situation, Mom would say I should let him play with it for a little while since I wasn't playing with it anyway. Okay, autistic brother or not, no kid likes hearing that. It was mine and I had a problem with only one little thing... he had it and it wasn't his. Mom tried to explain it to Tony but he still didn't like it. Dealing with mom was okay but then Dad would get involved and Dad for sure does not care about justice. Dad would come in the room and explain that he couldn't understand why I wouldn't share my toy with Tony. There was one thing that I could never understand and no one seemed to care about it. Why did I have to share with my brother when my brother wouldn't share his toys with me? Again, it was "Alexandra, he doesn't know any better." After a while, I felt like saying that sentence for them all. Of course, Tony won that one and I had to let him play with my toys until it was close to bedtime and time for him to give them back to me. The good thing was we only fought about toys or when he would mess something up in my room. I never started a fight with Tony verbally or physically and he never did with me. We never had anything to fight about because he was nonverbal and I never acted like I was better than him in games or anything like that. If we stayed out of each other's hair and didn't annoy each other, we never fought. Now that Tony is older, we fight a little bit. Not always, but he still doesn't understand "no" means "no" and he will keep asking the same question until you give him what he wants. That drives me insane! Mom and Dad tell me to have patience, but even they can't take him constantly asking sometimes. Tony enjoys listening to music. He started getting into it when he was about 16 years old. Before he had his own device with music on it, he would use mom's phone or try and take my iPod which always bothered me. If I remember correctly, I would hide it so he couldn't get it if I happen to be out of the house when he is home. I love my music also and listen to it a lot. My iPod touch is older, but I normally only use it for the music. It still works, but if the screen is on for a long time, it will die because it is old. When Tony plays music, he doesn't always let the song finish. He skips through songs constantly and keeps the screen going. Then when he leaves and I go to use it, it is completely dead. That makes me furious. The worst part about it is when Tony comes home, he eats snacks and touches the screen with his messy hands, so my iPod is not only dead but disgusting too. Now that we are both young adults, we know a lot more and certainly know what we are capable of doing, especially Tony. He isn't stupid at all. He knows more than we all think. He still asks for Elmo and Shrek, however, he really doesn't like Elmo and Shrek that much anymore. Yet, he still asks for it. We don't let him watch it because it makes him crazy and he starts to have a meltdown. We don't know what triggers it. For me, it can be Elmo's voice because now that I am older, I just think that Elmo is highly annoying. Tony will ask and ask until we put it on. I normally change his mind and give him a choice. I will say, "You can watch *The Lion King, Monsters Inc.,* or *Beauty and the Beast.*" Once I give him other choices, he chooses one. I think he knows how to annoy me more now than he did when we were younger. The hard part about the whole thing is that even though he is older, he still doesn't understand that everything can't go his way. I think as the sibling of an autistic child, I always thought that I should step in and help because for one, I was the sister and two, as I got older, I realized if something ever happened to my parents, I would be the next one in line to be there for him because I was the closest one next to Mom and Dad. My parents always told me to not worry and go out with friends or just go out and enjoy myself. I never really wanted to. I wanted them to know that I will be there to help and sometimes I was the only one. I think the fact that I always stayed home with Tony is how I became a homebody. A lot of times, when I was home with him, I would think about what other kids my age were doing, about where I could go with my friends or cousins, and about why I was given this life. I also thought this could be good for Tony and me to spend this time together. Even though Tony went to a school with kids like him, and had friends to do things with in school, I always knew, and I think Tony knows this too, that I will always be his number one friend and the person he can always trust to be there for him. Yes, I made the choice to help out with Tony and watch him for my parents so they can have a break, but in the end, if I have to choose going out or being there for my brother, my brother will always come first. Being a sibling to a child with autism is truly a blessing. Even on bad days when you think it isn't such a blessing, you still realize how important they are to have in your life. I never learned so much in my life and it was all because I was blessed with Tony. I always felt that I was given this life for a reason. Did I know this was the kind of life I would have? No, not at all. Are all siblings annoying and give each other a hard time about stuff? Yes, of course, whether they are autistic or not. When he starts to ask questions after you said no the first time, the next step is to just ignore him. That doesn't last very long, because he is still asking for something that he has his mind set on and he won't stop until he gets it. After a few minutes, I end up yelling at him, "SHUT UP! I ALREADY TOLD YOU NO." At that point, fuel is now added to the fire. For me, It can be hard to stay calm with Tony. When he throws a tantrum for whatever the reason it is, I can't do it, I just can't. He makes my blood boil and I don't know why. I love him and know him well, but I lose my patience with him too fast. That is how bad he gets on my nerves. I think I just don't like that he constantly repeats himself until my head hurts and starts spinning because he doesn't shut up. In the end, I end up getting yelled at by my parents because I lost it on him, but I can't help it. He constantly annoys me with the ongoing questions after he was told a thousand times "no." Mom and dad lose their patience with him too. After a while, after the tenth "no," you just don't want to hear it anymore. Afterwards, I feel really bad and go and see Tony to say sorry. Each time I would say sorry to him, I tried to explain to him that he can't keep asking after he has been told no and he needs to listen. Of course he says okay, but then he does it again. That is what makes me realize what his autism does to him. He just doesn't understand because of his disability. There isn't anything I can do about that besides live with it and do what I can for him and myself. I have walked away and out of the house, blasted music, and distracted myself from him and his tantrums. Even then, I can still hear him from outside or through my headphones. People would always say to me, you must be used to Tony's tantrums or they can't be that bad. I have heard that from friends, teachers, workers for DCF, Wheeler Clinic, and even family members. There was nothing that made me angrier than hearing that. I don't care who you are and what you think you know. If you don't have or live with a child with special needs, then don't tell me what it is like or assume you know. No one knows what it is like until you have lived and dealt with that child. It is the biggest challenge in the world not only for the parents, but for the siblings as well. It is hard to live a normal life, especially when you don't have a great support system from family. For us, we made it through with a lot of help. Most of the family always helped us, supported us, and checked up on us. Others were judgmental, critical, and could simply care less. All they would do is judge us for how we handled Tony and how we handled life in general. As a daughter and sister of a child with special needs, I saw that and it bothered me that my parents were treated like that. As the sibling of an autistic child, you start to notice how hard it is for your parents. I watched as my parents struggled, fought, and held it together on days when they really couldn't. No one knew how tough my parent's job was but me. I was there and I lived it for myself too. I had it hard, but it taught me a number of things like always be kind, respectful, and simply accept everyone no matter what. A little respect goes a long way. Everyone is battling something behind closed doors, so don't ever judge or criticize anyone. No matter how many times I yell, get mad, or get annoyed, I'll always have my brothers back no matter what. Raising an autistic child doesn't take a special family, it makes a special family.

Chapter 7
The Walk for Autism and Donations

In 2008, I was ten years old and Tony was seven years old. It was the first year we did the walk for Autism at Walnut Hill Park in New Britain, CT. It was a wonderful turnout and was by far the hottest day of the year. It was a lot of fun. Our grandparents, aunts, uncles, cousins, and friends of the family all came. There were a lot of us. I picked our team name and called us "Tony's Crew." We all wore green T-shirts that had the logo and Tony had on an orange T-shirt that said, "I'm Tony." The walk began around 1 p.m. on the first Sunday in June. It was very hot outside. Grandma Mary stayed home at the house to set up for everyone to come back after the walk for food. The walk was great. We had a big sign that we carried that said "Tony's Crew" on it with the Autism puzzle piece. Tony did wonderful and walked the entire time, but by the end, everyone was tired and had enough from the heat that day. Everyone went home to shower before they came back to our house. Back at the house, family and friends came back for a great afternoon. Dad blew up an inflatable pool for us and we used it to fight the heat. The amount of money we raised was awesome. We were so happy and appreciative of everyone's love and support they gave for Tony. In 2009, we did the walk again and it was the best thing I looked forward to all year. This time, it wasn't very hot out which made the walk a little more manageable than the year before. Tony always has energy, and we always tried to find a way to help him blow off steam every day. The walk was great for him and he really enjoyed it. The giraffe was there from "Toys R US" and Tony got a big kick out of him. He went over to him and hugged him. It was a wonderful experience for me as a kid and being the sister of a brother with Autism. I look back now and think walking in support of my brother and all of the other wonderful children diagnosed with Autism, was one of the greatest things I ever did in my life. Just like the previous year, everyone went back to the house after the walk where we ate, had fun, and appreciated all the help, love, and support everyone gave us. Tony was always included in everything and everyone came out on that day just for him. As a kid, I had a fun day with my family. Now when I look back, I realize everyone did it for my brother and that is what is so important to me. That same year in

2009, we had a pasta dinner on our own to raise some more money for Autism Speaks. We did it in late July, about a month after the walk, and it was another wonderful turnout. Dad, Mom, Grandma Mary, Uncle Jack, and Papa Dave were a big help in making the event happen. Grandma obviously made the pasta. She cooked all day long from early in the morning. Mom and Dad got the decorations and other supplies. Uncle Jack also helped us cook the pasta, and Papa went from place to place, shop to shop, and company to company, handing out cards for the benefit to raise money. People came pouring in. There was music, a raffle, and pasta for everyone. It was a great time for a wonderful cause. We felt good to do that and to raise a lot of money for Autism Speaks. In August of 2009, our grandfather Papa Joe passed away and Grandma Mary sold her house to move in with us. We stopped doing the walk after that because we remodeled our house in the spring of 2010. I came to realize something as I got older and Mom had once told me she believed the same thing as well. We stopped donating to Autism Speaks for one reason. The money goes towards raising awareness. That is great, but I wish that some of the money went towards actually helping families in need who have a child with autism. My parents and I know that sometimes there is very little help, not just from family, but from the state. There are families with autistic children, who like my brother, aren't potty trained even as a teenager. They have meltdowns and tear the house apart. They like to blow off steam and can run off when no one is looking. They need help/care 24/7. I think Autism Speaks is a wonderful program and we have met a lot of people through the walk, donations, and much more. And they all went through the same thing as we did raising Tony. The reason we just decided to stop is because we believed that the money donated should go to help families who really need the help. Not just any help, but help as their child grows up. Things like services, group homes, social security, in-home support, and more major help for when the child grows up to become an adult. We learned a lot more about Autism Speaks and what it is through Tony's teachers and paras at school. It was great that we got to learn and see not only what we go through every day, but what other families deal with every day on a regular basis.

Chapter 8

Reasoning for Medications and the Side Affects

I am sure medication and autism are not a surprise to anyone. Most autistic children are on some kind of medication to help them with different reasons. A lot of kids with autism today start on medication at a young age, depending on the reason, like how bad the autism is, and the child as an individual. Tony is on a few different kinds of medications and they are all kind of for the same reason which is to help him stay calm. Fortunately, Tony wasn't on any medication for something serious. He doesn't have seizures or any other serious conditions that affect him besides his autism. Ever since he was young, he wasn't the best sleeper at all. As he got older, his sleeping got worse. He would go to bed at 11 p.m. and be up at 5 a.m. every day. After a while, Mom and Dad knew something had to be done, because his sleep schedule was exhausting. When Tony was 8 years old, he was put on his first medication. The doctor prescribed him Abilify, which can treat Bipolar Disorder, depression, and Tourette syndrome. The medication can also treat irritability associated with autism. The medication made a difference and was a big help. We always gave it to Tony around 8:30 p.m. when it was near his bedtime and he would sleep a good eight to nine hours depending on the night. If he was having one of those days, we would give it to him earlier to keep him calm and get ready for bed. His sleep schedule got better and easier for all of us. I forgot how old Tony was when he was put on his second medication, but it was around the time when he was eleven or twelve years old. The problem was his tantrums. How do we control them and mellow him out quicker? How can we even try to prevent them from happening? That was when Tony was put on a medication called Clonidine. It helps treat high blood pressure. Certain formulations can also treat ADHD and Cancer pain. This medication allows your blood vessels to relax and your heart to beat slowly and easily. Tony was given this to help with his meltdowns and try to control them a little easier. It took a couple of weeks to see an improvement in Tony because the medication had to get into his system. Once it did, we noticed it took the edge off. He seemed to concentrate a little better, and was calmer. We noticed it especially on the weekends when he was home all day. He took one Clonidine in the morning when he woke up and one with his Abilify before he went to bed at night. I don't ever remember Tony with normal blood pressure when we went for our yearly doctors' appointments. I am assuming Tony has and always had high blood pressure from being on Clonidine, because he still had meltdowns despite the fact he was on it. I firmly believe that no medication can make Tony not have any meltdowns, due to the fact that he can't communicate why he is mad or upset and that is normal for him. To at least have my brother's tantrums to be less violent, loud, and controlled, is easier for my parents and for myself to handle him every day. Tony was put on a third medication shortly after the Abilify and Clonidine. This medication was also given to him in the morning and night as well. He was given Torpiramate. It was the last drug he was given. In total, he took these three meds every day. Torpiramate is used alone or with other medications to help prevent and control seizures. It is also used to prevent migraine headaches and decrease how often someone can get them. Tony is on Torpiramate because of the side effects to one of his other medications which can cause seizures. Thankfully, Tony has never had a seizure. So, Tony's daily medication routine is in the morning and at night. He takes his Clonidine and Torpiramate in the morning when he wakes up and both again before bed along with the Abilify. Luckily, Tony never had any problems with any of these medications and never gave us a hard time when it was time to take them. All of these meds worked in different ways to help Tony more with his tantrums, sleeping, and focusing. Of course he is also prescribed Lorazepam (Ativan) to take when needed. It is a drug that can treat seizure disorders like Epilepsy, but is also used to relieve anxiety. Mom would always cut Tony's Ativan in half and give him half of one when he had a severe meltdown. It usually works quickly to start calming him down, depending on how bad the meltdown can be. The Ativan was always in the cabinet just in case it was needed and we also packed it in Tony's bag for when we were going someplace so we had it on hand. You learn very quickly to take precautions because no one knew how he was going to act. Mom wasn't so sure at first about putting Tony on these medications. She said it was something she didn't want to do to him. She realized later on that it can be a lot of help. We had no choice but to put Tony on these to help with his tantrums and sleeping problems. Of course, when

Tony had one of his meltdowns, whether it was big or small, we had no idea what triggered it to happen. Other than Tony's prescribed medication, we also gave him over the counter drugs when necessary. He took cough medicine when he was sick or for the stomach bug, unless our pediatrician prescribed him with medication for being sick. When Tony starts having a meltdown, mom either gives him half of one of his Ativan or if he was hitting his head during his tantrum or banging it against something, sometimes Mom would give him an Ibuprofen and a Benadryl to help him calm down. Mom and Dad would use their judgment because sometimes we would think he is just having a meltdown because something hurts him. Depending on his tantrum, we would either give him Ibuprofen and Benadryl or/and Ativan. If you are a parent of a child with autism, don't be afraid to ask the doctor about medications to help your child. My parents were against it at first but realized what a great help it was. It helped Tony not only calm down during his worst moments, but also helped us control him better. Sometimes as a parent or sibling, you come to a breaking point. There were many times me or my parents watched Tony and you could only listen to blood curdling screams

and banging on doors and furniture for so long. It is
something no one will understand unless they live with it. I
don't care if you once witnessed it. Try living with that
every day and not knowing when it will happen and how
bad it will be. Tony still has meltdowns, but when you
know you have something there to take the edge off and
help prevent it from getting worse, it is a lot easier to deal
with. There aren't too many side effects to Tony's meds
other than the Abilify which makes him want to eat. That
is why we always had to lock up snacks and restrict Tony
from having them all of the time. It was a challenge,
especially when you have him behind you all of the time
asking for something until he gets it. Other than that, Tony
didn't have serious side effects that we had to worry
about. We learned having a child with autism is worth
asking the doctor or psychiatrist questions about
medications that can help him. If you are a parent of a
special needs child, don't be afraid to ask. It will help both
of you.

Chapter 9

Do Patience Even Exist?

Okay, patience is something not many people have. There is not a lot of patience in my house and no, I am not talking about my parents and I having the patience. I am talking about Tony's non-existent patience. Tony doesn't have patience at all and that only makes me lose my patience. Really the bottom line is nothing makes you lose all your patience more than listening to someone without any patience. My brother never ever had patience. I don't think he was even born with it. When he wants something or knows we are going somewhere, he just sits there and needles you every minute. Asks over and over again about whatever it is he is waiting for. I learned how to spell certain trigger words from a very young age. I would say things like, "Dad, are we going to the p-o-o-l?" If you ever said the word "pool" in front of Tony, but weren't really taking him to one, he would be on top of you asking, "Pool? Pool? Pool?" I spelled out a lot of things that I knew would haunt me if Tony ever heard me say it. Things like, "cake," "pool," "bye-bye," "bathing suit," and other words that we just knew would get him started and would escalate into question after question, unless you can find a way to distract him, which was not always easy. His one track mind was always there and when he wanted something, he wanted it. I didn't get it as a kid. I would sit there watching my brother ask and ask and ask. I would sit there and think to myself, listen, I want another cat, a dog, and I want to go to Disney World once a month, but we can't have everything. Even swimming, ice cream, or cake. It is called life. I still think that, and not because of my brother, but people in general. And dear God, when Mom said "wait a minute," you waited a minute. Tony wouldn't give you the chance to even say "wait." We had many relatives who had pools. Grandma Mary's pool was the one we were always at. However, when Grandma moved in with us, we would mainly go to Uncle Paul's house to go swimming in his pool. We are always welcome there and Tony knew the house, so it was easy for us to watch him there and relax. On a hot summer weekend, Mom would ask if we wanted to go swimming at Uncle Paul's. Of course, we always looked forward to going there. Tony and I were typically always the first to get ready. Once we were ready, Tony wouldn't stop until we got in the car. He would ask, "Pool?"and I would say, "Yes, you need to wait for Mom and Dad." Two minutes later, he would ask, "Pool?" And it would keep going on and on until we got in the car to go. I don't know if Tony repeatedly asked because of his autism or because he really just didn't believe us until he actually knew we were going and he was getting what he wanted. After the third or fourth time I heard the question, my blood would boil and I would lose it. I would say, "I mean come on Tony, enough already! Just sit down and wait for when Mom and Dad are ready." I can't remember the amount of times I would have to walk away from him to calm down. I know he is autistic. Again, I don't need that talk from anyone, but when you have to constantly listen to him over and over every two minutes, autistic or not, it gets annoying after the fifth time. Most of the time, I would stay in my room and lock my door because he would go around the house if someone said no to him and he would ask the next person. I will admit, I don't have patience with a lot of things. I lose it very quickly, but when it came to Tony having no patience, it made me lose mine and I never found it again. If I had a dollar for every time he said "cookies," "pool," or "Shrek" in a day, I would never have to work. When I stayed home with him for my parents while they were out, and I would hear him coming out of his room down the hall, all I can think was, "great... what is he going to haunt me for now?" If it was going to be something that he and I both knew he wasn't supposed to have, I knew the question was going to just haunt me for the next forty-five minutes. If you have a sibling with autism and you can relate to this, just know something, do not be upset or mad at yourself for freaking out and yelling at your sibling. You can only listen to it for so long. Sometimes the best thing you can do is just walk away. I have done it many, many times. I've taken long walks outside, locked myself in my room, and just went outside to get away. I figured out when I got older that if I am calm and relaxed, I can handle my brother a lot easier. If I am just as wound up as he is and out of control, I will flip out and make the entire situation worse. It was a different scenario for Tony and me. If I was told no or wait, I did what I was told. Why? Well, because Mom and Dad were in charge and you listened. If you told Tony "no" or "wait..." then forget it, you ruined his day. Of course back then, I never understood why he wouldn't listen. I knew I had to listen to Mom and Dad or whoever was watching us or was with us. Tony didn't understand that. I had no choice but to accept that and deal with it because there was no way for anyone to explain to him what is right from wrong. Tony never really learned right from wrong because of his autism. Yes, he listened when he absolutely had to, but when he wants something, he wants it right there, right now and if it isn't in front of him within the ten times he has already asked for it, then you are about to witness World War Three at its finest. Now that I am older and look back, I think I have more patience now because of my brother, however, some days are still questionable. In the end, you learn that many other kids don't know. That is just part of having a sibling with special needs. It is a challenge, a big challenge. It causes you to think all of the time. As the sibling, you are just learning as much as your brother or sister. There are some days that are easier.

Chapter 10

Don't Explain Yourself

Having an autistic brother means you always get asked questions. Not just from strangers, but family and friends too. You get asked things like, "Does Tony always do that?" "Is it hard to handle Tony?" And the one question that drove me nuts, "how would it be if you can get more help?" They are just questions that make you feel pressured, awkward, and sometimes embarrassed to answer. When I was younger, I got those questions from my friends or other kids I met while we were out. Sometimes, I would even get them from a family member. Most of the time I would say, "he acts like that because of his autism" or "he is different than me because he is autistic and he can't talk." I used to sit at family functions or events and listen as Mom would talk about how Tony acted and how she and Dad handled him. I would sit and think, "why are they asking mom that?" For me, it was hard to live with it at home and I always thought answering people's questions was sometimes harder. As I got older, the questions bothered me even more and most of them were asked by my own family members, not even friends or strangers. It became highly annoying because they would constantly ask and not understand why it was the way it was. I would respond with, "well, that is how Tony likes it and the way he does it and that is just it." Tony does his own thing differently because he was different. Some family members would ask, "Does Tony eat steak?" "No, Tony doesn't like steak." "Well why?" Okay... what else do you want me to say? Every kid is picky when it comes to food and children with special needs can be very picky. Tony didn't eat much and we just knew what to do and what to have on hand for him. Then you get, "Why don't you try getting him to eat it?" That is when I start to get annoyed. Of course we try to get him to eat it, but after a while you don't want to try anymore. It gets tiring sitting there going back and forth with him trying to get him to eat food that we know he doesn't like. We even tried saying if you eat this you can you have this after and even that didn't work. This was because it was Tony's autism. He had different taste buds than the rest of us. For us, as long as Tony ate, and it was something healthy, that is all that mattered. When I would go home and lay in bed, I would think why did I even answer that question? Why did I bother? I know my brother and how he acts and why he does it. I live with him. I watch his actions and his mannerisms every single day of my life. As a kid, I might not care or know about Tony's actions because I didn't really pay attention. However, I got to know my brother better over the years and if anyone knows how to handle him, watch him, and be there for him other than my parents, it was his big sister. Even at times when he annoyed me. I am no expert on Autism or the background of it, but I live with it and learned how to deal with it. It is not just the questions that we are asked. It is also people trying to tell us how to handle and live with Tony. If you have a child with autism, it isn't a problem at all. It is nice to talk to other families with an autistic child and hear what they do to help their child. When you don't have an autistic child or don't have any children at all, then I don't want to hear it. Unless you live with it, don't talk to me about it. Even when people say, "Did you try this?" or "What about this?" Okay... Why are you asking me when you don't know or live with my brother? The other problem is not all autistic children are the same. Tony is low functioning, making him different from other children with autism. The hard part was not just having to explain Tony or his actions, but also explaining my life in general. I also would get asked why I live the way I do, why do I do what I do when I am home, and other things that I handle differently than most people. I handled my stress in different ways and the one way I still handle it to this day is walking while listening to my music. I do it in the kitchen where it is open and I have the most space, and I do it for a good amount of time. My friends and family would ask why I do that and after a while I would say, "I handle my stress in my own way." And that is the truth. If Tony was annoying me, I would put my headphones in and just zone out. I feel like I am in a whole other world when I do that and that is the whole point of it. To escape from reality somehow with nowhere to go and just try and relax. I also would lean on the comfort of my pet cat. Sometimes in your stressful moments, you don't really know what to do. Pets are great comfort and can relax you in your hardest moments. Sometimes during one of Tony's episodes, I would sit on my bed with her and pet her and talk to her as I was trying to calm down. That was how I handled it, but even if I didn't live with an autistic child, I don't feel as though I have to explain myself of why I live my life the way I do.

For those who have a sibling with autism, and any parent with an autistic child, don't ever feel as though you have to explain yourself. First of all, people shouldn't be judging you or your child and second of all, you know why you have to do what you have to do and that is all that matters. Just do the best for you and your family. I used to always explain myself just to get my point across to people. That this is how we handle it and why. Don't ever, ever feel like you have to explain yourself of how you take care of your child because no one knows. No one really knows what it is like to live with that child more than their parents and siblings. Don't explain yourself! You know in your heart what you have to do and that is all that matters. My parents and I know in our hearts what we have to do for Tony and in the end that is all that matters to us and Tony.

Chapter 11

Our Search for Help/Services

This is probably one of the biggest challenges families with autistic children face. It took us the longest time to get the help we really needed. It was a long, stressful, heartbreaking, and painful journey. I think my parents always had the thought in the back of their minds, since Tony was young, what was in store for the future and where would Tony end up? For my parents my dad's mom, Grandma Mary, was their biggest support and helper with Tony. My brother adored her and knew he could always get his way when he was with her. Grandma passed away unexpectedly in our house of a heart attack. Both of us were devastated along with my parents. I was 15 years old and Tony was 12 years old. I remember the night grandma died and people flooded our house I pulled mom aside and my first question and reaction to it was what are we going to do about Tony? Who will watch him? Mom promised me that we will figure it out and the whole thing will work out just fine. Tony went to school during the day which was a big help for mom and dad. The weekends we somehow worked out but it was much more difficult since grandma passed away. Either we went to Uncle Paul's house, Uncle Dave's house or to see Papa Dave and Grandma Kathy. Papa Dave, our grandfather on our mom's side, was diagnosed with stage four colon cancer the year before Grandma Mary died. We tried our best to break up our weekends. We would often times have company over, which was much easier than taking Tony out. A year went by and it was 2014, in April mom ended up breaking her ankle in two different places and was wheelchair bound for 3 months. A very kind and supportive teacher of Tony's, Mrs. Remington, encouraged mom to seek more services for Tony. Up until that point she tried but she always felt as though it wasted more of her time than it was worth. She felt like she had to jump through hoops each and every time gaining little if any reward for her efforts.   It was that year that my mother was able to secure a place for Tony in a state respite house nearby. It allowed Tony to attend for 5 days each quarter and was run similar to a camp with planned activities and outings for the guests to participate in. We would drop him off on a Thursday night and pick him up on Monday. It enabled us to get away for a few mini vacations. Traveling with Tony became increasingly difficult as he got older. He tended to wet the bed 5 nights out of seven, which made hotel stays difficult. My parents sent him 4th of July weekend in 2014 which was also my 16th birthday. It was great for us and for Tony. It enabled us to enjoy a little bit of time together without having to worry about whether or not Tony was okay. We were a little nervous just because we were dropping him off and leaving him not knowing how he would react or take it as we left him at a place he'd never been to before. One of the very kind state employees that was helping us in the house a little assured mom that she worked at the house and Tony would be fine.   It was a great and relaxing weekend for us knowing Tony was safe, with kids like himself, having fun, and with great staff and a nurse on hand as well. The house was very nice, the bedrooms were spacious and the yard was well equipped with swings and the like for the individuals to play on. Tony didn't give us a hard time either. He wasn't upset we left him and transitioned pretty easily. He happily waved us good-bye and ready for his weekend adventure. It was also a vacation for Tony. He was with kids his age and participating in all kinds of fun activities. Don't get me wrong, when Tony was younger, and a little easier to handle we enjoyed going on vacations. Once he got tall and out grew the stroller, outings became increasingly difficult. He was much too big for anyone to carry him if he decided to have a full blown temper tantrum. When that happened he could be very loud and destructive as far as property went. Because he was like a time bomb and we never knew what would trigger him, it was a little risky taking him out and we didn't want to take that risk. This was his own little vacation and to be honest I was quite jealous myself. I would love to go away with my friends at that age with no parents. Tony was excited when we went to pick him up and had a great report from the amazing staff that looked after him there. My parents and I were extremely pleased, he did so well and it made us feel good knowing his stay was enjoyable for him. Being able to send him there took some of the pressure off mom and dad. Finding care for Tony when we had to go to family events, a wedding, a birthday party, a funeral was not always easy. Knowing that he had a safe place to stay gave us piece of mind and allowed us to look forward those things rather than dread them. Before that one of us usually stayed behind to take care of Tony. Fortunately Tony was very adaptable and loved people. Because he was unfamiliar with them he didn't really have any temper tantrums during his respite weekends either. It gave us some hope that one day maybe Tony would move to a group home and be happy. It was mom's hope for the future because she was concerned about the responsibility I took for him at such a young age and she wanted to be fair to both of us. Tony consumed most of her time, attention and energy. We were able to utilize respite four times a year. We took that time to either go away or to get stuff done at home that we couldn't with Tony there or even just do things as simple as go out to eat. Tony was like a time bomb in a restaurant and often times we would order and end up having to ask to have them pack the food to go. Mom was very fortunate to meet some very kind, helpful individuals throughout our journey. Two of whom worked for the state Department of Developmental Services. They were assigned to come to the house and take Tony out for a walk for an hour or so a few times a week when she broke her ankle. They helped us find out more about this respite service through the state and it helped us tremendously. Tony at the time was attending a special needs school about 25 minutes away from our house called ACES. It is located in North Haven, Connecticut and is a school for all special needs children. Tony's teachers and caregivers there suggested that we look into more help through Wheeler Clinic and DDS (Department of Developmental Services) to see what they could offer us because Tony was starting to get hard to handle and was very qualified for services. Mom started to look into services but was discouraged time and time again. When she broke her ankle, she grew more and more determined. Tony and his everyday behaviors were the "normal" for us because we were so used to it. A teacher of his pointed out to my mother that when she described Tony's issues, she had a tendency to minimize the severity of them because she was so used to dealing with them on a day to day basis. That is when mom realized she needed to push harder to receive assistance with Tony. Grandma Mary was my mother's right arm when it came to Tony and since she passed just working became increasingly difficult because child care for Tony always fell back on me. No one else was really willing to take it on. Before receiving any state services we had to go to contact Wheeler Clinic first. Mom wasn't thrilled because she had them out to the house before Grandma Mary died. And while she and Grandma

Mary adored the social worker, who was such a kind man, more of her time was wasted. My mother was working from home, Tony would wet the bed most days even with a diaper on so she was faced with three to four loads of laundry, sheets, comforters, matrass pads, before her feet hit the floor in the morning. Grandma Mary helped her with a lot of that. The social worker that would come out to the house would insist on meeting with them once a week. Mom said is was like having someone over for coffee, they would chat each week and he was more than pleasant but it accomplished nothing and after a time my mother and Grandma were no longer willing to meet with him because it was just a big waste of time she didn't have and nothing helpful came from it. This time, they came out to our house the first couple of times to get to know us and Tony and collect all of his information to try and gain a better understanding of him. We had two different people come out to the house each week. After a while it got very annoying. I am telling the honest truth, it annoyed me and half the time I stayed in my room. I don't even know why they came out. Once again, they didn't help us at all. One of the main issues we were dealing with at the time was Tony escaping from the house. Mom and dad alarmed all the doors but he still managed to escape from time to time and they were growing increasingly concerned for his safety. We live on an extremely busy street and Tony would sneak out and go to all the neighbors' houses, especially the ones who had pools. My parents were hoping that they could offer some assistance in fencing the yard in or part of the yard at least. They were such a joke. Again, this is where I say to people, you don't know unless you lived with it. Week after week they would come out talk to us again and basically do nothing. Then this one week one of the ladies came to our house with these laminated signs that said "Tony Stop" to hang on our front door, back door, and garage door. Now I am not a teacher or a doctor but I knew one thing about my brother... They were never going to stop him. He was non-verbal and unable to read! So supposedly Tony is supposed to walk up to the door read that sign and say, "No I have to stay in." Wait, there is more. After she hung up those signs on all our doors, she then had this colorful caution tape like police officers use. She proceeded to string it around the entire perimeter of my back yard and that was supposed act as a barrier and keep Tony in our yard. Normally when these people came out, my parents did most of the talking.

My mother had more patience with them than my dad. Unless I was asked a question or mom asked me a question I tried to keep my distance. I also didn't want to answer some of their stupid repetitive questions. They really agitated me because they just didn't understand. Now my mom, Tony, and this lady are walking around the yard, stringing up the tape. Mom was trying her best to be respectful and polite. Far behind them I followed. In the distance, with my arms crossed, shaking my head, and saying to myself, "my parents have been fighting for help all this time for this?" Now, we go back inside and dad comes home from work and looks around then looks at me. I shook my head and just said, "This is sad." The meeting for the day is over and the lady leaves the house and I am still standing there off to the side silent with my arms crossed. I had nothing to say, I didn't know what to say or do. I was very, very aggravated. The lady left and now we had these signs on every door saying "Tony Stop" and this bright yellow caution tape all around the yard making it look like a crime scene. A few days went by and Tony walked out of the house about 23 times and walked through the tape about 30 times. Like I said I am not an expert on Autistic children especially because they are all different but, if you think that a Stop sign and caution tape is going to keep a 6 foot 2 inch, 230 pound kid in the house… You're crazy, there are no other words other than you are crazy. Dad has very little patience as it is but after a few weeks he finally threw the signs out and removed all the tape and. Family and friends would come over and ask what is with the signs and the tape? We told them that Wheeler Clinic put them up for us to help keep Tony in the house. No joke, every single person in my house laughed, and laughed and laughed. It infuriated my mother that the state was funding these programs that were such a complete and utter joke. Every person who asked laughed because it was the dumbest and craziest thing that they have ever heard of. Now that I look back, why did we bother? Why did they come out and even do that? I am sure they were well paid individuals. Whoever these programs were funded by … What a waste of money? I mean if I was a worker trying to help a family with an Autistic child I would have fought as hard as I could to help them get what they needed to keep their child safe. I would a have gotten the state to help the family out as much as possible. They couldn't get my parents a fence for the yard. I really don't even think that they even tried to.

The services they offered were no help what so ever. Tony was still escaping and even brought back home by the police a few times. I would never show up at someone's house to try and help them with their low functioning autistic child with stop signs and yellow caution tape. My mother was growing more and more discouraged. If I was that lady, I would have been very embarrassed to even do that to someone. Even if Tony was 6 feet tall, any kid, person, or animal could run right through the tape and Tony did. What was the point? Now when this lady came to our house and saw the signs and tape missing, she asked us where it went. This is where I had to keep my mouth shut! Mom said, "it didn't work, there was no point. My son can't read for one and doesn't care if there is tape around his yard if he has his mind is set on leaving the yard, he is going to leave the yard." My mother is the best mother ever. She is very calm and can handle anything. If the lady asked me where it all went... I would have said, "DID YOU HONESTLY REALLY THINK THAT A STOP SIGN AND TAPE WERE GOING TO STOP MY BROTHER OR ANYONE FROM GOING OUTSIDE! TONY CAN'T READ AND ISN'T AN IDIOT EITHER! HE WAS SMART ENOUGH TO KNOW IT WASN'T GOING TO HOLD HIM

BACK." Again, this is why mom does most of the talking. The other lady that came out to our house was even worse. They would visit on different days, were a big waste of time and but were still no help to us at all. The other lady would come out and ask questions that used to make me want to say bad things. Mom handled them very well and she did stand her ground a few times with them. This one would ask questions like, what kind of help are you looking for Tony? Mom and dad both said, we would eventually like to have Tony be in a group home with other kids where he can get the services and care he needs. She would ask, why do you want that? My parents deserve to have a life and not have to take care of Tony until he is 80 years old. My parents explained to both workers that is wasn't fair to me anymore. I was his only caregiver besides my parents. Obtaining child care for Tony even to go to work was impossible. Who wants to watch a 6 foot 2 inch individual that still wasn't completely potty trained. Caring for Tony and meeting all of his daily needs was exhausting. Mom and dad also explained to both workers that they didn't want to have me take care of Tony if and when something happened to them. They felt I deserved to have a life of my own now that I was older. Life for all of us revolved solely around Tony's needs since his diagnosis. I often volunteered to home and watch him so they could attend special occasions, work related events, etc. They weren't willing to allow me to take on more responsibility for Tony than I already had. Now, of course my parents and I still wanted to play a huge part in Tony's life and I always told mom and dad I would always be there for him when they aren't and make sure he is being taken care of. The extent of Tony's tantrums and the property destruction he cause were the icing on the cake. My parents could no longer meet all of Tony's needs 24 hours a day 7 days a week. The tantrums, the potty training, the laundry, the escaping the house, the property destruction, mom especially was at her wits end. They were basically taking care of a grown toddler with no end in sight and little if any help from anyone outside of our household. Mom wasn't looking to get Tony placed right away but she was hoping by time he was at least 18 years old she would somehow manage to be lucky enough to have him move into a group home. She was continually told it was highly unlikely that would happen. They informed her he would need to be at least 21 and even then there was a huge waiting list and his chances of being placed were pretty low. One of the ladies who came out to the house, repeatedly asked us the same question, "Well, what would your life be like if you could get the help you need?" After several months of the same line of questions, Mom finally snapped one day at the lady and I proudly sat witnessing it with a grin from ear to ear on my face. I mean come on, why would you ask my parents that question over and over again knowing that you couldn't fulfill that need for them anyway. She'd already explained numerous times that they don't actually provide the caretakers you need. They merely hound you to beg family and friends to do it for free. This woman knew my parents were struggling day in and day out and they weren't helping them in anyway. My parents entertained these individuals week after week for several months, fighting to get help for all of us and every week this individual brought up the same question. My mother finally said to her, "Are you trying to torture us?" The women was startled by my mother's question. My mother looked her dead in the eyes and said, "Sarah, each and every week, you come into our home and you ask me what will it feel like if you had someone to care for Tony and you didn't have to worry? What will it be like to know Tony is safe? Yet after months Sarah, you have yet to help us accomplish any of those things. If you are not going to help us, then damn it Sarah, stop asking me those questions. What purpose are they serving?" The woman stopped asking those questions and I think that was the last time my mother allowed her to come to the house. She was beyond fed up with the nonsense and didn't appreciate her time being wasted. I will tell you what it would be like: It would be great to know Tony was safe, being cared for, and enjoying activities with kids like himself every day without having to worry about him. We could call, pick him up and have fun with him and continue to play a major part in his life. Knowing he was being well cared for so we could relax a little and not constantly be on the edge would be a huge relief, even so my mom could simply work. I watched him several days after school if mom couldn't be home. I give mom a lot of credit, she is a strong, brave determined woman who wasn't willing to take "No" for an answer. I would have lost my cool, my patience, and everything else by then and would have called it quits. Mom had other ideas and decided she needed to approach things differently. She was now angry and determined to get Tony the services he and we as a family needed. Mom started recording and documenting Tony screaming, fist pounding and property destruction during his tantrums. She and took pictures of stuff he damaged in his room and the rest of the house as well as the bruises or cuts he inflicted upon himself as a result of throwing his tantrums. Wheeler Clinic came out to the house and we showed them everything. Still nothing, it got us nowhere. It was very disheartening that they lead you to believe they can help, yet all they do is basically they collect a bunch of data and do nothing. Wheeler Clinic provided us with nothing and when they were all finished they gave us a packet of papers about Tony and his disability. To be honest, I couldn't wait for them to stop coming out to our house. I was more than done with all of it. I could have written out that packet myself about my brother, his disability, and more and it probably could have got me further. The lady that came to the house and asked all those crazy questions was very serious, hardly cracked a smile, and couldn't take a joke. One day my parents jokingly said, we can always just duct tape Tony to a chair if it makes him stay put. She responded with, "I am a mandated reporter you know." My mother told her if she wanted to report us to knock her socks off. Despite many difficulties with Tony my parents never once hurt us or laid a hand on us in the sixteen year up to that point. My parents always had a good sense of humor about things and that wasn't the first time a so called person who was supposed to help us threatened them with the fact that they were "mandated reporters". Mom remembered it and used it against them later. After Wheeler Clinic drove us crazy and didn't help us or even try to help us we went to plan B. Tony's teachers in school had a lot of students who received a lot of home services and monetary help. His teacher, who was so nice, encouraged mom not to give up. She informed my parents that some of the families receiving services were pretty well off and had more than my parents did yet they persevered and received assistance with their kids. She knew Tony was more than qualified to receive services and how severe he really was because she worked with him on a daily basis. She encouraged mom and dad to call DDS and look into their services. We ended up getting in-home services for him. For us, it was a great start and also gave us a big break. Once mom filled out all the paper work and got it all straightened out We had people come to the house every day to take Tony out or just stay home with him and help us with him around the house. Someone would come every day after school and participate in activities with him. On the weekends either one person came, or one would come for 5 hours and another one would come for 4 or 5 hours. They were all such wonderful people and were great with Tony. Each person came out to the house whatever day they were scheduled and introduced themselves to us and met Tony. The lady who was the head of this program was a very nice person and would send mom a schedule every month or week of who was coming for Tony and what time and day. Mom would print the schedule and put it in the kitchen so we knew the time and person. Tony really enjoyed it and looked forward to it each day. It was nice for my parents and me as well. I didn't have my license at the time and even if I did I would have to wait 6 months before I could drive with Tony in the car anyway. However, my parents both worked and I had school and my friends to go out with, none of us had the time to do all that with Tony. They would take him for lunch, the park, the store, bowling, and other places for him to just burn off steam and get his energy out so when he came home he was relaxed. That didn't always happen, sometimes Tony came home in a bad mood. So, everyday mom would leave money on the table for them for Tony's lunch and I would get Tony ready. He looked forward to it, he never gave them a chance to come in the house, and he just wanted to go out. This went on for a while and certainly helped us a little more but, we still dealt with the constant bathroom issues, tantrums, damage, and headaches from trying to best care for him and keep up with his everyday needs. In addition my parents had to provide money each day for them to take Tony someplace and that wasn't easy on them financially either. It was very tough and I sat back after a while and started to lose hope. I thought we would never find the help we really needed. Having people in your house all the time solved one problem and created another. The sad part was the DDS wouldn't help or even try. There are families out there in the same situation as us who need this help and care. They are struggling to provide for their children's needs 24 / 7. There is nothing that breaks my heart more than to see families struggle. We were one of those families. I know what it was like, the frustration, the heartache, and the feeling of being trapped.

Chapter 12

Mom's Heroic Phone Call

Teenage years are challenging, very challenging. No, not challenging like your typical teenager. Parents say their teenagers drive them crazy and it gets worse. Blah, Blah, Blah. I hear it all the time. When your teenager is going through puberty and is severely autistic, doesn't talk, and has constant tantrums worse than a toddler then, we can talk about it. Tony was a very, very hard teenager to handle. I know going through puberty doesn't help and is hard for him because he doesn't understand what is going on. Again, just like when he was a kid some days were just better than others. As dad would often say, "when Tony is good he's good, when he is bad, forget it." His tantrums got worse and worse every day. I can feel the tension building in the room just by looking at him, knowing he was going to start and wondering how long it would last this time? Why can't he learn how to relax? When he became a teenager I started to notice my parent's patience was running out. They weren't losing patience so much because of Tony they were losing patience because nobody would help us. I was in my sophomore year of high school and I wish there was something I could do. I felt helpless, upset, and saw no hope for my brother. I saw him staying home with my parents until they couldn't do it anymore and I would have to take over full-time like they did. I saw no future for my parents. I thought why? Why should they suffer? Can't someone at least do something? I really wanted to help mom and dad out so, I wrote a letter to my state Senators explaining who I was and what situation my parents and I were facing every day and that is was starting to get worse. I spilled my heart to them and told them everything we have been through. Can you guess what happened? Yes, you're right nothing! Absolutely nothing, I didn't get a response or even an acknowledgment. It pains me and breaks my heart that there are thousands and thousands are services out there for these kids and they won't tell families how to go about getting them. We knew there was help out there, there is plenty of it. You just have to think outside the box and figure out a different way to go about it. It is the hardest thing to do, it is so much work that is exhausting, challenging, annoying, and above all sad. I sat in my house each and every day watching my parents fight for my brother and get nowhere. They fought and fought for more services for him, writing letter after letter, email after email, and making phone call after phone call. There was no doubt in anyone's mind that Tony was qualified for much more than we were receiving for him. His teachers knew it, his paras knew it, my parents knew it, and I knew it. The problem was finding the help and getting it for him. I don't know what was going through my parents minds and how they handled this on their own when they were alone. I never asked and never bothered them about it. I would ask mom questions about the situation and ask if she thought we would ever be able to get the help we so desperately needed. I don't think mom was so sure herself at the time but she kept telling me that it will work out and we will get the help we need. All I knew was I felt helpless, I wanted to help, I wanted to be involved. Tony was my brother too and I love him more than anything on this earth. I want the best for him and my parents. At this point I didn't care about me, if I had to build a house with an in-law apartment attached to take care of Tony I would do it for my parents. Mom and dad were getting tired and slowly losing their patience. Tony's care was a 24 hour 7 day a week commitment. His teenage years took a toll on us with his loud and aggressive behavior, having to change his clothes 4 or 5 times a day because of his bathroom issues, the non-stop laundry because he wet the bed every night due to his sleep medication. It would certainly help him sleep but he couldn't wake up to go to the bathroom (when he was smaller mom was able to lift him out of bed before she went to bed and make him go to the bathroom but now he was just too big for her), and on top of it watching Tony's weight which was a side effect of one of his medications. That was the hardest thing for us. His medication made him constantly eat and we always watched what he ate the best we could but, when you are already having a bad day and he wanted something to eat he wasn't really supposed to have and he keeps asking continually even when you say, "No". And then he starts having a tantrum over it where he sometimes would punch holes in walls or break windows, in the end you're finally like forget it! Eat it! Eat everything in the house, I don't care! His care was getting harder to maintain for mom and dad and they couldn't give him the extra help that he really needed. To just watch mom and dad struggle each day fighting for their child, who they loved and cared about more than anything, was the saddest thing I ever witnessed. It was getting worse before it got better and my parents still couldn't get the help they really needed. For one thing, mom kept thinking about the Wheeler Clinic lady telling us over and over "I am a mandated reporter." Every time this women came to our house she said it to us. One day in July of 2015 mom used this to her advantage. Tony came home from summer school in a mood and nothing was changing it or making it better. I knew it wasn't going to be a good night from the time he came home. Well, I was right… The night was about to take a turn for the worse. Something triggered Tony like any other day and he started one of his tantrums. I sat in my room like I normally do trying to ignore him the best I could. All of a sudden I heard this loud bang that literally shook both of our bedrooms. I got up to see and Tony slammed his bedroom door so hard that it shifted the entire door frame out of alignment. I walked away from it and sat back on my bed, a few seconds later I heard mom pick up the phone to make a phone call that was probably the hardest decision she had to make. Mom called Tony's behaviorist and I heard her say, "You are a mandated right?" He obviously responded, "Yes." Mom explained to him in detail, what just took place and said to him, "I am declaring myself an unfit mother. If something is not done about the situation in my home soon as I may either hurt myself or my child. Now that I have told you this, you are mandated to call DCF and report it ... Yes?" The behaviorist had no choice, my mother turned the tables on them. She used the very thing they'd been threatening her with time and time again to get the help we so desperately needed. Mom was in her right mind at the time, while extremely upset, she had no intention of hurting anyone. She knew it was the only way she was going to get somewhere. I don't know what the individual on the receiving end of the phone said to her, but I knew my mother had enough. I stayed in my room and waited, I didn't yell, scream, or move. Mom and Dad had to go to a DCF hearing where they pleaded their case. The case worker that got this time knew her stuff and got things done. Shortly after that hearing, mom came in my room one day and said, "There is a group home in Bristol with an opening for a new kid." Tony will be placed there by September." I sat there speechless and heartbroken. That's what it took to get my brother placed? That is what mom had to do to help her son. So, there was a group home out there with an opening, there was help, there was a solution but, they only offer those solutions to those who claim total incompetence. Mom went through so much. All the fighting to get Tony what he needed, the non-stop calls and emails, the endless stream of individuals in and out of the house on a daily basis. In the end though, my mother had to make a risky decision for herself and her kids and completely trust that it would all work out for the best of everyone involved. I am grateful for her every day. That phone call could have gone much worse. At the time Tony was 14 and I was 17. They could have taken Tony and me away from my parents and throw mom in some nut house. We were and still are beyond grateful Tony is in a great group home with a great group of people, kids and staff. It was the best thing we did for all four of us. It was a rocky road. What they didn't explain to us was that Tony would be taken from our house by DCF as if he were a victim of child abuse even though they knew he wasn't. It was a DCF protocol and at that time they didn't have different protocols in place for families like ours. One of Tony's favorite in home support staff members had to drive Tony to the group home because he had to be taken by a third party. That individuals, a big burly guy that Tony adored, had tears streaming down his cheeks when he came to the house. He told mom if he had any idea that morning that he was going to have to be the one to bring Tony, in that manner, where he was being treated as an abused child, he would have called in sick that day. He was sick to his stomach. They didn't allow my parents unsupervised visits for 6 weeks and after that they had to adhere to a schedule of short visits. At one of the meetings my mother told the DCF coordinator that she would volunteer her time to help them put protocols in place for children like Tony so that no other family would have to suffer the way we did but you know how government agencies are. It fell on deaf ears. The way Tony got placed was sad and something no parent should have to go through. When it comes to your kid and the best for your kid you just do what you have to do. To all parents and siblings who feel helpless, just know there is help out there somewhere. You have to just fight for it to find it even if it means making a heart breaking phone call like my mother had to do. It is very sad and all Autistic children, their parents, and siblings deserve more. They deserve to receive the help they need and the extra support in transitioning from teenager and then to adult. My parents did the best job they knew how raising my bother and I. They did a great job. The help they finally received was well deserved and it gave them a little bit of freedom to do what they wanted to do free from worry about Tony's safety and well being. We are all so grateful that we get to see Tony whenever we want and do fun things with him now that they couldn't do before. In the end, it was the biggest blessing knowing Tony is safe and controlled by people who are trained and supportive of children like him. They have patience with him because they work in shifts and are not solely responsible for him 24 hours a day, 7 days a week like my parents were. Tony is living a great life with friends of his own who are all different each in their own unique way, he gets to participate in fun activities that we could never do with him because of work and school. On top of that, he has learned invaluable life skills to assist him in his everyday life and allow him to become more independent. Tony will never be able to live on his own but for the 3 of us, to knowing he is safe, well taken care of, and learning new things day after day makes us so happy, relaxed, and also confident that anything could happen if you believe it could and you trust that it will work out, even if it means taking a risk for your loved ones. Times were tough, very tough, we went through so much, but in the end when you know there is light at the end of the tunnel it lifts you up and reminds you that things always work out and that you can do anything you set your mind to. When something is meant to happen for you, it will happen and no one can stop it. It will all work out in the end. It was tough for us to get there, but we did. Whether mom planned to do what she did or she snapped in that moment and made the decision to make that call, I don't know. Whatever the case may be, she made it work and was finally given the help and services that my brother and we as a family so desperately needed. Mom's phone call that day changed our lives for the better and I am grateful for that today and every day of my life.

Chapter 13

The Transition

The great thing about all of this was Tony was and still is a great adapter. He can adapt anywhere and get used to anything which helped to make this transition go a lot smoother. Tony was supposed to start high school at Aces High School, but mom wanted to start him right away at the school he would go to through where he was going to be placed. The service and schools were called "Oak Hill." The problem was they were giving mom a hard time about that. Mom wasn't trying to cause trouble by any means, but it made sense to have Tony start at the school he will attend for the rest of his school years in his new program. Why have him start at Aces High School for two weeks and then move him to Oak Hill and confuse him? Well, the fight about this didn't last long at all. Grandma Mary worked at Southington High School as a paraprofessional for 25 years and my parents had good connections with the people on the Southington Board of Directors. A few of them were best friends with grandma for years. All mom and dad had to do was make a phone call to them to explain the situation and that all we wanted was Tony to start at his permanent school. They were so wonderful. I am not sure what they did or said, but Tony had a private van from Oak Hill pick him up every morning for school and drop him off at home before the day came where we had to move him into the group home. He loved his new school and still loves it. The staff and teachers are wonderful. I have never met such nice people. I say all of the time, especially from living with it, it takes a special person to take that job. For about three weeks or so Tony was going to the school in Bristol through Oak Hill until the time came to place him. During this time we were running around between Tony and papa. Our grandfather (mom's dad) was dying of stage 4 colon cancer. It was a difficult time for all of us. I was very close to papa and at the same time, Tony had to be placed in a group home. For my parents and myself, especially my parents, we knew that this was a good decision for Tony, but at the same time no parent wants to give up their kid. It was a difficult moment. Before Tony got placed, he was still given the in-home support with the people who came to take him out for the day, which was a huge help for my parents during that time. September 7, 2015 Tony was ready to start something new in his life. It was also something new for my parents and me. I got home from school before Tony and started to help mom load up the car with Tony's clothes, stuffed animals, and belongings. Tony got home from school and he was in a good mood. He saw mom and me packing and it didn't seem to faze him at all. Dad didn't want to take the ride because he wasn't sure how Tony would react once we left. I was a little scared myself. I knew that this was the best decision for Tony and for ourselves, but if he wanted to come back home with us there is no way I could let him stay there. I was a little scared, but looking back at his respite vacations, he did very well and I was hoping that this would be no different. We had the car ready to go and Tony was ready. The big problem that also bothered mom and dad was that Tony had to be brought to the home by a third party. One of the people that worked with him through the in-home supports took him to the house and my mom and I followed. The reasoning for this situation was that they had no protocols for the situation we were in which was that we couldn't continue to give Tony the care and services he needed. The only way he could be placed was as if he was removed by an abusive household. Mom tried to sit and talk with them about this to make a different way for children like Tony to be placed because they couldn't get the care they needed and were not being abused. They didn't care or listen to mom's idea. The entire situation was just sad. The house and people who worked there were absolutely wonderful. Tony had his own private room to fit all of his stuff. There were a total of 6 boys there. The home is for kids 12 to 21 years old. When the kids outgrow to 21, they get placed in a house for adults with special needs. Mom and I stayed to put Tony's clothes away and make sure he was comfortable and all set in his new room. The house also had a kitchen, living room, a big bathroom, and an office for the manager of the house. There are four bedrooms. Two kids share two of them and the other two bedrooms have one person in them. There is a big, fenced in backyard with swings and a deck. Coming from me, I thought it was a great place and I knew Tony would adapt well like he always does. Mom and I were getting ready to leave an we said good-bye to Tony. He did very well. It didn't faze him at all. The one thing we had a problem with was his manager. She would not work with us no matter what the situation was. It was a simple "no" each time something was brought to the table and it was starting to aggravate all three of us. Tony was placed a month before papa passed away and mom wanted to take Tony home at least three times a week to go see him before he got worse. The manager and behaviorist said, "If you can take him that many times a week, why can't he live at home?" First of all, mom still wanted to see her son along with dad and I too. Even though he was in a home, it wasn't stopping us from taking him home to spend one on one time with him. Secondly, we only took him for three to four hours. We didn't take him for the whole day and during the week we couldn't take him anyway because he had school. This went on for a while and on October 7, 2015, papa passed away early that morning. It was heartbreaking for all of us. Within the month, we placed Tony and lost our grandfather. It was a very stressful time. I felt bad for mom trying to work with a schedule to see Tony and on top of her giving him up, she lost her father too. After going through all that nonsense and finally figuring something out where we can still see Tony, he comes home every Thursday after school for at least four hours. He also comes home on Sundays for basically the whole day. It works out for everyone and that is the schedule Tony is used to. It was still hard for us because we could work with anyone and about anything, but his manager at his home was tough. My parents were definitely strict with certain things and I understand that she is running a house with six kids in it, but why be so strict? They were teenagers like I was. They don't need their rules to be that strict like they are little kids. She gave us problems with picking Tony up and having him dropped off as well as many other things. It got to the point where I couldn't go get him anymore because I was so annoyed. Other than that, we were really blessed to have found this place and have Tony be a part of it. Tony was able to do things that every teenage kid likes to do. He plays basketball every Monday, September to December, and we get to watch him play. He also plays baseball in the springtime. On the weekends, he goes bowling with his friends. They do all kinds of activities in school during the week as well. The transition was great. I was afraid at first to let him come home because I didn't think he wanted to go back. I thought he would beg to stay home, but he didn't and still doesn't. We tell him when it is time to go and he gets ready. He loves coming home to visit, but never gives us a problem going back which is wonderful. I am very grateful to see how comfortable he is at his new place. I think the hard part about the transition for me was I kind of felt like I was an only child. I missed having someone else there to hang out with or watch a movie with. It kind of hit me at first and it brought back memories of Tony and I as kids playing games, playing outside, watching movies and having fun. Even when Tony was older and harder to handle, I always took advantage of going outside to either swim with him or go on our trampoline or anything he was in the mood for. I realized this decision my parents made was a good decision for all of us and I am not sure what would happen if Tony wasn't placed by the time I had to go to college. Now that I look back, I was always there for mom and dad and if someone was not home in time to get Tony off the bus or watch him, it would have to be me. This could not have happened at a better time for us. My parents didn't have to worry anymore and neither did I. When we get to see Tony, we can enjoy him and do fun things with him and then bring him back home knowing that he is in a good place. I saw a big piece of stress lifted off my parent's shoulders. It was getting hard for them and I knew I didn't want to see them still taking care of their kid when they are seventy and really can't do it anymore. I learned that you have to take the good with the bad. Yes, my parents had to give up their kid and yes, I feel like an only child and sometimes I'm lonely without Tony around, but it was the right decision that was made. Tony is in the best place and has overcome a lot of things. One of the biggest changes that we noticed is his eating habits. Tony eats just about anything now and yes it is scary. I almost fell out of my seat when I saw him eat salad, chicken, and steak! It was amazing to see that. They really work with him at the house to get him to try new things and do new things. For his caretakers, it is easy because that is their job, but for us it was hard. You lose patience after a while sitting there trying to get him to try something that he just doesn't want. We even bribed him with other things, but it wouldn't work. I am sure that is exactly what his caretakers are doing. Whatever they are doing it worked and he eats almost everything mom makes when he comes home to visit. Another thing that somewhat improved are his tantrums. I don't know what they deal with at the house or how many tantrums he has a week there, but they normally don't call mom about his tantrums unless they are really bad and he either ends up going to the hospital or they have to restrain him. We have gotten a couple of calls, but not many at all. I would say we get like three or four a year if that. That is his caretaker's job and for us to not have to deal with it all day, non-stop anymore was good for us. Tony even stopped having fits every day because he is always kept busy at the group home or at school. The transition worked for my parents as well. Papa died a month after Tony was placed and it was the first wake and funeral where my parents didn't have to worry about finding someone to stay at our house with Tony. Mom and dad were finally relaxed and not worried about Tony. He is in a safe place with the right people and that is all that matters to mom, dad, and me.

Chapter 14

Onto Oak Hill School

Tony switched schools three times. He adapted well at each school he went to. For the group home, he had to obviously attend their special needs school called Oak Hill. His house was under the Oak Hill special education company as well. Oak Hill School is a private, state approved, special education school, meeting the needs of each individual student. They offer a 12- month community-based education program for day and residential students. The schools are located in the state of Connecticut. Each student receives a highly specialized program emphasizing skill development in the areas of: functional academics, daily living skills, fine and gross motor development, communication, social skills, self-advocacy, and community participation. The schools serve students from moderate to severe disabilities from ages 3 to 21. Tony obviously will stay at the school until he is 21. He learns everyday life skills and is also taught behavioral skills as well. When he was having a tantrum or about to, he would show his teacher and caretakers why he is mad using pictures. He has goals and objectives in school and Mom gets a quarterly report about his progress. A couple days a week, he stocks shelves at our local Petco Pet Store. Other days, he goes shopping to get food and supplies the house and school may need. Once a week, he goes around with someone to ask the teachers and staff if they want coffee, tea, or hot chocolate. Then he makes the orders and delivers them personally to each person at school. Keeping him busy is one way he has progressed so much because he is getting around and out and not sitting in the house on the computer or in front of the television all day. Tony progressed at his goals and objectives over the past year. The first couple of years, he was in his group home and was getting used to the school, teachers, and the way he has to learn. He enjoys cooking, science projects, going out into the community, and of course, vocational activities. Tony can be very receptive when following directions and completing tasks. Tony's behavior has improved, but he can still scream and bang loud enough to wake the dead. Tony's behavior intervention plan has been developed based on a functional behavior assessment. The target behaviors being tracked at school and at his home are bolting/elopement, head hitting/hand banging, aggression, property destruction, tantrum, screaming, and perseveration. He is very good at following his schedule, however, there have been a few incidents of all target behavior over the quarter and Tony currently requires one on one staffing at school due to aggression, bolting, and tantrums. As for the staff, teachers, and caretakers, they still don't know like we do what triggers Tony to act like this or what fires him up. Other than watching something on his tablet or television that makes him get crazy, we don't know why he gets triggered out of nowhere. When he lived at home, he was usually yelled at by us after losing our patience and we would give him his medicine to calm him down. Tony has a Behavior Intervention Plan where they are tracking his bolting, self-injurious head hitting, physical aggression, property, tantrums, screaming, and perseverating. Proactive techniques in his plan include a structured daily schedule, with the opportunity for breaks, and free time following the completion of academic tasks. He does best in less stimulating environments. Tony is still on a one on one supervision due to his behaviors. He also has a history at school of breaking glass. Oak Hill really has helped and improved my brother. Oak Hill School sets the standard in empowering students to learn through meaningful, functional, and innovative educational experiences which build self-advocacy, independence, and reinforce the dignity of students using comprehensive trans-disciplinary supports. Oak Hill's vision is to teach every student through creative, innovative, functional instruction and meaningful activities, so that each student will become more independent in his or her life. Tony has become much more independent since he has been going to Oak Hill, however, he will never be able to live on his own because of his low-functioning autism. Even with that said, he can do things on his own very well like making his bed, taking a shower, doing the dishes, helping out, and more. Of course, he is monitored at the group home as well and still requires a one on one person with him because of his tantrums and aggression. The group home occurrences of bolting, hitting head, property destruction, tantrum, screaming, and physical have decreased since he has been there, not that Tony doesn't have his moments because he does. Normally, if he has one during the week, they notify us when they drop him off for his visit or tell us if they see us at the house. However, at school, the staff works to remain consistent in schedule and expectations to target these behaviors. As of last year, staffing in the classroom changed from daily rotation to weekly rotation, so more often Tony has an expectation of who to expect to work with day to day. At school, behaviors are generally short in duration and redirectable verbally or by cue in most cases. In any case, where Tony needs to be directed out of space due to target behavior, he is successful at returning to schedule when provided with a new task that he has prior success in within a new classroom area. Tony does not have any documented target behaviors while in the community during school hours. I give these staff members all of the credit in the world. I was never ever once able to redirect Tony during a tantrum verbally. It just never happened. He wouldn't listen and I would just get as mad and frustrated as him because he wasn't listening to me. These people are just beyond wonderful and special. They own their job and are great at it. Once Tony got comfortable and used to his new home, school, teachers, and staff members, he did wonderful. He still does, despite his tantrums and aggression he still has due to the autism and because he can't talk and express himself for why he is feeling the way he is. As Tony continues his schedule with the home and with school, they are keeping up and looking at recommendations to keep Tony independent and well behaved as best they can throughout each and every day by utilizing his IEP objectives to decrease target behavior across all settings. They continue with his behavior intervention plan, and build on coping and communication skills, especially focusing on visuals. Overall, Tony has adapted beautifully at Oak Hill housing and schools. He has become more independent and more focused on things. His listening has improved somewhat, but of course in the end he still has his moments like every person does. We couldn't be happier with his teachers and caregivers; they are truly remarkable with him.

Chapter 15

Home Visits

It is very relaxing and quiet without Tony home. I can concentrate on homework, my writing, and my journaling. I do miss seeing him though and he gets to come home on Thursdays after school and Sundays for the day, unless he has something planned with the house or he is having a tantrum or getting antsy. He has his own routine when he comes home and usually if mom has time, she makes meatballs or sausage for him, which are his all-time favorite. Tony will arrive and when I answer the door, I wave to his caretaker, or whoever it is that brought him home. I ask what time they are coming to pick him up. Then Tony will come in and depending on who is over, I make him go and kiss and hug everyone hello including Mom and Dad, wherever they are in the house. After that, he goes into the pantry to get a snack, typically it is always pretzels. Another favorite of his is Smartfood popcorn and Mom buys it for him once in a while if she is shopping the day he comes home. Tony doesn't have a computer anymore because he broke it when he was living at home during one of his tantrums, but when he comes home to visit, he has a tablet he uses to watch his movies on YouTube. He actually watches a lot of old videos from when we were kids like *Lady and the Tramp*, *Bear and the Big Blue House*, and more. We don't let him watch Elmo because it makes him agitated and triggers him to a tantrum. I mean, I always thought Elmo was annoying anyway. I am not so sure why it makes him crazy, but we know what he can and can't watch, so we try and plan before he comes over. Most of the time, he finds Elmo somehow. I don't know how. Tony also likes to be outside if it is nice out. He will take his tablet on the back porch or go outside and blow bubbles or just run around the yard to blow off steam. If I have time, I take him to the park where he goes on the swings. Then I take him to Dairy Queen or something like that afterwards. His home visits normally always go well. Sometimes, he seems a little more anxious than normal, and we have to redirect him and have him walk away from his tablet and have a glass of water, then let him go back. He listens and behaves for the most part. For us, we had to get used to Tony's schedule and decide when is the best time to take him and when isn't. We learned as we went along that sometimes when we took

Tony after vacation or on one of his long activities, he was out of routine and that triggered him to have a tantrum. Tony goes away for one week in August to camp at a beach for special needs kids. The first time he went away, we took him home a few days later when he got back. We then realized to give him a week to get back on his normal schedule. The first time we took Tony home after his vacation at camp, he was out of sorts and not in his normal schedule. When he came home, he was okay at first, but something triggered him and I think it was the worst fit I ever seen him have in my life. Dad always used to say when Tony was young, and would throw a tantrum, he wanted Tony to look him in the eye one day and say "fuck off" because Tony could never talk and Dad always thought about Tony talking and saying that during one of his tantrums. We never noticed this until Tony reached his teenage years, but when he is having a tantrum, he speaks full sentences, clear as day. You can understand everything he is saying. Mom and I think it is the adrenalin that goes through him when he is having a tantrum that makes him speak clear fluent sentences. That day he came home after his trip, we sat down with him trying to calm him down. He wouldn't calm down for anyone including me. Mom asked me to sit with him to see if he'll listen to me and relax, but he wouldn't even look at me. He was not all there. The tantrum really just took over and then he started saying fluent sentences. Well, I gave up and Dad sat down next to him to try and calm him down. Dad tried talking to him, "come on Tony calm down, it's okay." Tony looked at Dad dead in the eye and said "get the fuck out!" It was clear as day. Dad looked at Mom and me and said, "Oh my God, he finally said it!" I know it sounds crazy that we laughed that Tony said that, but he could never talk and he never said it intentionally to anyone ever. We always found humor in every bad situation, because that's all you could do. Afterwards, Dad did yell at Tony and told him not to say that. He didn't seem to be calming down. We couldn't medicate him because number one, we didn't have his medications anymore because he didn't live with us, and two, we couldn't because Mom wasn't his legal guardian anymore. He would be under DCF custody until he turned 18. Then he would back into my parent's custody where they can make decisions for him. Well, Tony calmed down a little, but Mom ended up calling the house to have someone come pick him up because we were afraid to take him in the car to go back home. One of his caretakers came to get him and Mom called the house that night to see how Tony was doing. From now on, when Tony has camp, we wait a week until we take him home for a visit, so he can get back on schedule. It did make a difference the following year. Again, he can't tell us what it is that is bothering him and we think it is just because he is off schedule and just needs to get back on it before he comes home for a visit. We were told that Tony is off schedule the following year, and they had some trouble with him going back to school and doing his normal routine. Other than that, Tony never really throws big tantrums at home too often. He sits on the couch with his tablet and watches his favorite shows. He knows enough to help himself to any snacks he wants or food in the fridge that Mom and Dad made. He also likes to listen to music on his iPod. He has a lot of favorite songs, some of his favorites are "Suspicious Minds" by Elvis Presley, songs from The Wiggles, Disney songs, "Brown Eyed Girl" by Van Morrison, "You Shook me All Night Long" by AC/DC, "Rock and Roll All Night" by KISS, and more. He likes all kinds of genres, artists, and albums from the 1960's and on. If Mom is all caught up on her work, sometimes we take Tony out for something to eat or to visit our grandmother depending on what was going on that day. If we didn't go out, Tony was just as happy to sit home and play on his tablet and iPod. He would rather do that than anything else. They don't let him watch television all of the time at the house, especially during the week when he has school, so when he comes home it is a treat for him to play on his tablet. In the Spring and Summer on nice days, I take Tony to the park at my old elementary school down the street from my house to swing and do whatever. On Thursdays, Mom babysits our little cousin Jack who both Tony and I adore. He is almost three years old. Jack loves Tony and often asks for him. He calls him "Tono." Jack has his own tablet and they sit and watch their tablets together while sharing a snack. When Jack is over, I take both him and Tony to the park. It ends up being a win-win because they get tired out and burn off some energy. Although Tony isn't home every day like he used to be, his actions, attitude, and determination have gone farther than anything I have ever seen. I enjoy watching him with his friends at the house doing his daily chores and work. He seems happy to do things on his own and to be as independent as he can. Monday nights in the Fall, he plays basketball. Of course, they don't keep score, but the kids have so much fun. Tony was always great at all sports and I always knew if he wasn't autistic, he would become a football player or a basketball player because he was the perfect height. He enjoyed seeing us there to watch him play and cheer for him. Even at home, I see a difference in Tony. It makes me so proud to see him go farther and farther each year and to see him do things on his own. I am just proud in general that I am his sister. When it is time to go home, depending on who brought Tony home, we tell him it's time and he gets his stuff and kisses everyone good-bye like always and has no problem going back. When I bring Tony back to his house, he kisses me good-bye and goes to do whatever it is he does or is supposed to do. Now that he has a new manager, his schedule works out better for my parents and I because she now has it written down that Tony is dropped off after school on Thursdays and picked up after dinner. On Sundays, we still go pick him up around lunch time and someone comes to get him around 5 or 6 o'clock. His home visits are great and I think the four of us look forward to it, even though I am working on my homework or writing sometimes. I try to sit with him for a while. He is so into his movies and music when he comes home. He is just happy to be doing that while sitting in our company.

For those parents and families who have a special needs child in a home, be grateful that your child is in good hands. Don't look at it like you gave up. Look at it as if you and your child both have the freedom and care you both need. If you don't take care of yourself, then you aren't in shape to take care of someone else. It gets to the point where you did your very best and tried your very best. There comes a point where you can no longer help your child with the services they need. Be proud that you were able to take care of your child for as long as you did. You now don't have to worry, and when you see them, you get to be with them without stress or worry. You can do fun things with them whenever you want and know that they are safe. For me, I enjoy Tony's home visits and I am glad that he is happy with the decision that Mom and Dad made as well. The only thing that is important to Mom and Dad and his sister is that he is happy, content, and safe.

Chapter 16

Thinking about Tony's Future

I always thought about Tony's future and where it would take him, and me as well. I wasn't sure at first where the future would take the both of us before he was placed in the group home. I would hope that there would eventually be some help to my parents or to me if it were up to me to take Tony in my own hands and take care of him. It kind of scared me and it was something that I always thought about in the back of my mind. I always knew I would be there for Tony no matter what the situation was or where he would go. I knew that if he ever needed anything or anyone to be there or make a decision for him when Mom and Dad aren't there, it would be me. I also always knew Tony looks up to me. I know he can't talk and tell me how much he cares or loves me, but I don't need him to tell me that. I know he knows that I will always be there whether he annoys me or not. I knew that my parents were working hard to make sure Tony has the best and supportive future. I knew that God would help guide my parents to work something out. I believed that everything would work out the way it is supposed to and it did. Mom and Dad did what they did so that Tony wouldn't fall on top of me. However, we have talked about it and I told my parents they won't have to worry someday when they are not here. I will always be there for Tony and checking on him to make sure he is alright and that he still comes home for visits. Tony's future from here on out looks wonderful. He is always working hard and excited to start something new all of the time. Thinking of Tony's future also makes me think of my future as well. I want Tony and the rest of the world to know that having an autistic sibling makes you so special to have such a gift. A gift from God that not only teaches you a lot of life lessons, but gives you hope for the future, hope that people will be kinder and caring and to have less judgmental and critical people out there in the world. In the end, that autistic sibling of yours brings more peace and love into this world than anyone else. I think about what Tony will be as an adult in his 20's, 30's, 40's and so on. I think about the things that will come to his mind one day when our parents aren't here. I think about what goes through his mind now and if he could talk, what would he say to me? I think about his future a lot and I want it to be as great as any other kid in the world. He deserves the same future that I will have, that other children will have, and what any other special needs child will have. Every child growing up with special needs wants to be just like all the other kids. They want to move out, become as independent as they can, and be with kids like them and their age so they can do what every teenager and adult wants to do, live their life. Mom and Dad have thought and talked about eventually moving down South. Mom said that she would maybe do 6 months down there and 6 months up here, however, we don't know for sure. We might even be able to move Tony wherever we go and into another group home, but only time will tell that. Now that Tony is over 18, he is back into Mom and Dad's custody where they can make decisions for Tony for what is best for him. I have not been to any meetings for Tony, however, my name is on the list and I am power of attorney if something happens to Mom and Dad or they can't make it to an important meeting for whatever reason. I can go for Tony and make the decisions if I have to. Tony is the smartest kid I ever met. He knows who is there for him and who isn't. He knows when something isn't right or when someone else is upset about something. He knows when someone is mad and he gives off that energy because it is all he knows. He may not know where his future will take him or what he'll do or where he will end up, but there is one thing I know and Tony knows. He will always have the best and be given the best. He will always get the best house, the best caretakers, the best programs, and the best services. My brother deserves the best in his future, wherever it takes him, like every child does. There is no doubt in my mind that Tony won't succeed in his future. He won't be able to get a job or get married or live an ordinary life like most people, but his attitude, personality, and smile will help him succeed in anything. My parents and I have gotten phone calls from his caretakers, teachers, and OT/PT teachers of what a wonderful and loving young man he is. That is all thanks to Mom and Dad for not just raising me, but raising a special needs child as well. They raised him to be kind, caring, and respectful from day one like they did with me, and that is what will help guide Tony to the best in his future. Of course, I will stick by him in that future during the good and the bad. Tony will eventually end up in a home for adults when he turns 21 years old. My parents get to look around and make the decision of where Tony should go and what house they think is best for him. Tony will no longer be attending school once he turns 21, but he will engage in other activities during the day like shopping, exercising, sports, games, and other activities to keep him moving during the day. Tony will get to see what adulthood is like. It isn't about just staying in school your whole life. I know he won't learn or be able to figure out how to write a check, balance a check book, pay bills, or get a job. He isn't in the high functioning category of autism to do that, but that doesn't matter. He will learn other things and participate in activities where he can learn new things and be with new people. All my parents and I want for my brother is the best in his future and I want to be a part of Tony's future. I will be there for his accomplishments, his awards, his good times and bad, and be there for him like any sister would. Tony has a great and bright future ahead of him. He is a sweet, loving, respectful, and smart young man. I can't see Tony's future or predict what it will be, but I know he will have a bright future just like any teenager will. Don't stress about your child or sibling's future. It will work out the way it is supposed to. Whether your child or sibling is in a group home or still living at home, their future will be just as bright as yours as long as they know they have your support and love to help them get to that future. Remember there is help out there for your child. There is help for them and for the family as well. If your child or sibling is qualified for certain services or care, fight for it, get it, and make sure it is what you want for them. The help and services out there will make your child's future bright and remarkable. They will be happy that they can do things like any other teenager can. They want to do the things we want to do and they deserve more than anybody. Do whatever you can do to make your sibling's future the best.

Chapter 17

Where Tony is today

Tony was placed in the Oak Hill group homes for special needs children in Connecticut on September 7, 2015. He will be there for five years in September of 2020. He has changed so much and is given the best care. He enjoys his home visits, visits at his sports events and games, and surprise school visits as well that my parents and I try to make every once in a while. My parents and I have been on vacation. I am now in college and I am working. We are able to do every day things that we couldn't do if Tony was home. I enjoy writing in my free time and write every day. There is now time and a quiet atmosphere and we are able to do the things we have to do every day. From hearing from Wheeler Clinic that Tony would never get placed until he was 18 or 21 if we were lucky, and to look at where we are now, is truly a blessing. Tony has improved and matured into a young man since 2015. He is in school until he is 21 and has a new teacher. He touches the hearts of people all over his school, his home, our family, and of course me. He is 19 years old this year and improving every day. Tony can make himself something to eat even if he puts the whole bowl of food in his plate. Sometimes I can catch him and tell him to take a little at a time. He asks for help when he can't figure something out rather than throw a tantrum. He helps out around the house if we ask him to help with something. He plays nice and interacts with all our younger cousins who come over and he enjoys every minute of it. He can't talk, or express how he feels, but I know he loves being with his friends and family. I can see it. We have great luck with all his helpers, teachers, and caregivers. We don't go more than a couple of weeks without seeing Tony depending on if we are on vacation, he is on vacation, or we have to cancel a visit for a family emergency, family event, etc. In 2020, we experienced something new. I had a trip to go to for Spring break down in Georgia with some friends. We were going to see one of our mutual friends who attended school down there. The Corona-Virus had just started to become noticed in the United States, but didn't get out of control just yet. I still went on my trip. I was gone for seven days and returned home safely. The day before I left, Mom got a phone call that we couldn't visit Tony and he wouldn't be able to come home until further notice because of the Covid-19 crisis. Of course, at the time, it seemed crazy to me and I wanted to see him before I left for my trip, but on the other hand, I understood completely why they had to quarantine the kids at the house. Some of the kids in Tony's house don't have the best immune systems and have a lot of health problems as well. Their safety is more important than anything. Thank God Tony doesn't have any health problems at all. He is autistic, but no life threatening health problems. If Tony were to get the virus, he is young and healthy and would be able to fight it off. I returned from my trip and Mom told me Tony was still not able to have home visits until further notice. We were told it would be until mid-April. I feel bad because Tony's mindset is like a child's and he doesn't understand why he has to stay in the house 24/7 and not be able to leave. I am not sure how it went because I wasn't there. We talked to Tony on the phone and explained to him that we would see him soon and that he needs to stay home for now because it is the best for him and his friends so nobody gets sick. Tony seemed upbeat on the phone every time we talked to him. Tony is not really a phone talker, he never was. He says "hi," "I love you," and "bye." That's about it, but he knows that it is Mom, Dad, and his sister on the phone saying hi to him and checking in to make sure he is doing well and having fun despite what is going on. We were informed that he is handling it the best he can like everyone else. We all have no choice but to deal with what is going on. His house bought games to play and they have been doing school activities at the house along with gym classes on television for them to burn energy. They are all taken outside during the day to run around and use the swing set in the backyard. I think it was eye opening for both Tony and my parents and I. Tony has had his days like always, but he made the best of it like we all had to. My parents and I look at the positive side through the whole thing and thought it through about not seeing Tony. Mom was comfortable with the fact that Tony did okay with going so long without seeing her, Dad, and myself. If we were to move or go away for a couple of months, Mom feels more comfortable to do it knowing he is okay. Like any person, if Mom and Dad moved, and I decided to stay in Connecticut, that is my decision as an adult and I will see them when I do and talk to them when I talk to them. They will be doing the same for Tony as an adult too. It is comforting for me too that Tony is okay without coming home, for in the future when I am all Tony has one day. He is so adaptable to everything and everyone. He turns 19 in May of 2020 and to me is a mixture of both my parents. He is tall like Dad and has a lot of Mom's traits as well. Looking back at old pictures, he looks a lot like our maternal grandfather Papa Dave. He has a lot of his features as a young man. His smile gets him very far. It has since he was young. All he had to do was smile and if it was very necessary, he got his way. His teachers and staff always tell us what a sweet, young man he is and that his smile makes everyone happy. Is Tony doing better today than he ever was? I can't say as far as his toddler years and childhood goes, because I didn't know any better or didn't really know about his autism until I was a little older. Is he doing better today than he was 6 years ago? Yes, I definitely see that in him for everything. His tantrums, his attitude, and just everything about him changed because Tony is now living a normal life that every teenage kid wants to live. He is going out with friends, doing activities, and more. Of course, he has to do this while being supervised and have a caretaker go with him, but that doesn't matter. He now can do things that I did at 15, 16, 17, 18, and so on. When Tony was home, I remember sneaking out of the house to go with friends, my grandparents, and aunts and uncles because I wanted to have time to myself and be a teenager like any teenager. I don't know what went through Tony's mind when I left the house and did things on my own, but I am sure Tony wanted to do the same and be a teenager like me. I'm sure he wanted to go out with friends, go to parties, and have fun. To him, there is no difference. If his big sister can do it, why can't he do it. I can't disagree with my brother at all. He can do anything I can. He knows how to swim, run, play ball, get a snack, pick a movie to watch, and more. Yes, he needs assistance and help with these things and supervision, but he deserves to do it, to have fun, and to live his life. I think Tony enjoys coming home to visit more today because he isn't stuck in his room all day on his computer or told "no" for everything he does, like trying to escape the house or take a snack. I think he knows now that he can go home. He can do what he wants and have fun, and then be able to go back where he knows he has chores and everyday things that he can do now. And he now has the services to do it all. I think Tony is doing great where he is in life and I have no doubt it will take him further to become a respectful, loving, young man. Oak Hill has been wonderful with him and we are beyond grateful that we found an amazing service like them to work with Tony with his everyday needs. These people are trained to work with kids like Tony. It is a career that they decided to take and they are beyond special people to work with kids like Tony. It is amazing to see so many wonderful people out there that are there every day for these kids for whatever they need on their good days and bad days. Thanks to these amazing and caring people for contributing to who Tony is today.

Chapter 18

One Proud Sister

No sister can be more proud of Tony and not just because he is a great brother. He may be different from other boys, but in my eyes, he is everything. I couldn't be more proud of the young man he has become and I couldn't be more proud to be his big sister. My brother is considered special needs. In my eyes, he is so special in so many ways. I had 12 years of school and took every class out there that I had to take, but still to this day, no one has taught me more important things in life than my brother. When I was small, I had no idea that one day I would be the sister of an autistic brother. I never knew my brother would attend a different school than me or couldn't talk or any of those things. I just knew I was going to become a big sister. Siblings of special needs children are very special. They have a gift. They understand and learn the important things in life and that is simply to be kind and accept everyone for who they are. I am very proud to say I have a brother with autism. I am proud to tell people that and to tell people that Tony is a great kid with a great personality, and is in a great place. I brag about my brother all of the time. Who wouldn't? Tony may have been born with autism, but that doesn't take away from who he is. My parents got judged and criticized by people in the beginning and again most of them were family. They were bashed about not going to family events or going to church and much more. As far as I am concerned, God accepts everyone for who they are. God created us. If my mother was given Tony, then God will forgive her for not going to church. Yes, we couldn't go out all of the time, take vacations all of the time, or do things with the family, but when we could take the easy way out with Tony, we did. It was just plain and simple. Rather than judge my parents and make them feel bad, why don't you offer them some help and support? We had a lot of family and friends who were and still are very supportive. Every time they see my parents they always ask how Tony is doing and say they miss him. When they see him today, everyone gets excited to see him and the young man he has become and how far he has come along since he was young. Everyone notices how much he has grown up and how much he has changed. As his sister, partner in crime, best friend, and guardian, I remember those who were there and those who weren't and I am beyond thankful for those who always supported my parents when they struggled with Tony. It wasn't so much me who struggled, it was them. Without Mom's strength and courage, Tony wouldn't be where he is today. I would have lost it in the very beginning. Mom went through a lot to do nothing but get help for her son which is what every parent wants for their kids. If your brother or sister is autistic, whether they are high functioning or low functioning, be proud to be their sibling. Be proud that you were special enough to have a sibling like them, because whether they are having a good day or bad day, and no matter how annoyed you are at them, they know and will always know that even on their worst days, their sibling is always there. There is no better person to have than a sister or brother, and for them, that is all they have who is super close to them besides their parents. Autism has taught more people in this world about acceptance and kindness. They aren't as quick as us or as focused as us, but they are slowly learning too. They are learning just like the rest of us are. It may take them longer and might not be easy for them to figure certain things out, but in the end, all that matters is that your autistic sibling has supportive teachers, paraprofessionals, parents, grandparents, family, and above all a supportive sibling who won't ever let them down. I am lucky and Tony is lucky, because I know that he loves me and knows that no one cares about him more than his big sister. He is lucky because I will never leave him or not be there for him. I wish the best for all families with autistic children. There is a lot of help out there and it is sad that these kids aren't getting more help. It is sad to see families struggle all of the time looking for help or not thinking there is help. My parents and I were once in your shoes. There is help out there and if your child or sibling qualifies for that help, ask around, fight for it, make it known you need it, and document everything your child does to help you receive that help and services. You and your child deserve the best and getting them help like we did with Tony can change their life and yours for the better. Being the sibling of someone with autism is the best role you could ever play in your life. You are just as special as your sibling. Don't be nervous to have a party with friends. If they have a problem with your sibling, then they aren't your true friend. Don't feel bad for getting annoyed at your sibling or yelling at them. It is okay to get frustrated. You are learning and trying to help them express themselves and you are learning as well to deal with that and live with it every day of your life. Don't be embarrassed at a family event or party when they start to act up. That is all they know and the family will understand. If they don't, that is their problem because they don't know how special it is to be related to your sibling. Don't ever put yourself down and think you are a terrible sibling because of something someone said or something your sibling did, but maybe you got blamed for it or because you can't handle them. It is a challenge that you face every day. You are doing the very best you can and that is all you can do. Don't be anything but proud that you were chosen to have such a special sibling. At the end of the day, all that matters is that your sibling knows you are there for them on their good days and bad days. Yes, those bad days could also affect your day too, tantrums can be stopped, crying can decrease, and anxiousness can be calmed. It is calming and comforting for them to know you are just simply there for them. I am a proud sister of one awesome brother. A caring, kind, loving, and happy boy. We may live very different lives and see things differently and think very differently, but Tony is something that will always be special to me. He has taught me that having a sibling with autism is very different. He made me realize that life doesn't always go the way you want it, especially when your sibling doesn't get their way or get what they want. He may be the reason why I have little to no patience and he may be the reason why I get nervous so easily, but he is the main reason why I am who I am because I learned at a young age nothing is more important than to just be kind. You don't know what someone is going through or what their life is like. Everyone faces their own challenges, so just simply be kind. Be nothing but proud because you should be proud. Tony has my heart and I have his back always.

Sibling Love

About the Author

Unlike many children, Alexandra lived her life with a younger brother with autism. It was a challenge for her and only got more challenging when she got older and realized the tiring, stressful and long days that went along with being a sister to a brother with autism. Alexandra certainly didn't have it easy growing up as a child, but nothing in life ever bothered her. She believed that life is what you make it with people who are fun, supportive, and caring. Alexandra learned to keep her friends close and have the best times whenever she can, whether it was a big vacation or just having friends or family over for dinner. She loves her family and always puts her loved ones first regardless of what she is going through. Alexandra questioned about growing up and what would happen in her future. She questioned if one day she would have to step up and be her brother's caregiver. She always thought about her future and wanted to do nothing but make a difference. She always loved to write from a very young age. She wrote all kinds of small stories and enjoyed free writing time in school. Once Alexandra graduated, she realized writing was one of her passions. With autism being a big topic today and so many children and families affected by it, Alexandra decided she wanted to share her story with the rest of the world and to especially families like hers. She was so dedicated to sharing her story with other children in her shoes so they know they are not alone and should be nothing but proud to have an autistic sibling. Alexandra believes that reading is a very important skill set as well as a tool used by children, teenagers, and adults alike. There are books on nearly every subject and we are lucky to live in an age where books are right at our finger tips. Books help us be or do or have almost anything our hearts desire. Alexandra is interested in all kinds of book and enjoys writing about anything and everything. As a personal story from a sister that grew up with an autistic brother, her goal is for this book to help siblings in that share the same role as her, that feel the same way she always felt, and who should know that they are very special people. Alexandra does what she feels in her heart she has to do and does it. She stands for all kids with autism and special needs and believes they deserve to live a life like we do. Maybe some can get married and some can't, maybe some can have kids and some can't, maybe some can have a job and others can't, but no matter that child's situation they should be treated with the same respect as everyone else and should be able to be independent as much as they can. Alexandra believes that children with autism or any kind of special needs deserve the best and should receive the services and help they need and qualify for. Parents and siblings deserve to have a normal life knowing that their child is in the right care and can become as independent as they could. No parent or sibling should have to worry about that child or their future. If you have been informed of services for your child or think your child is qualified for help, find it, fight for it, and make it known your child's life matters just as much as any child in the United States and around the world.

Other books by the author:

Camelot... What It Was and How It Ended

Why is My Brother Autistic?

We stick  together

through it all!!!